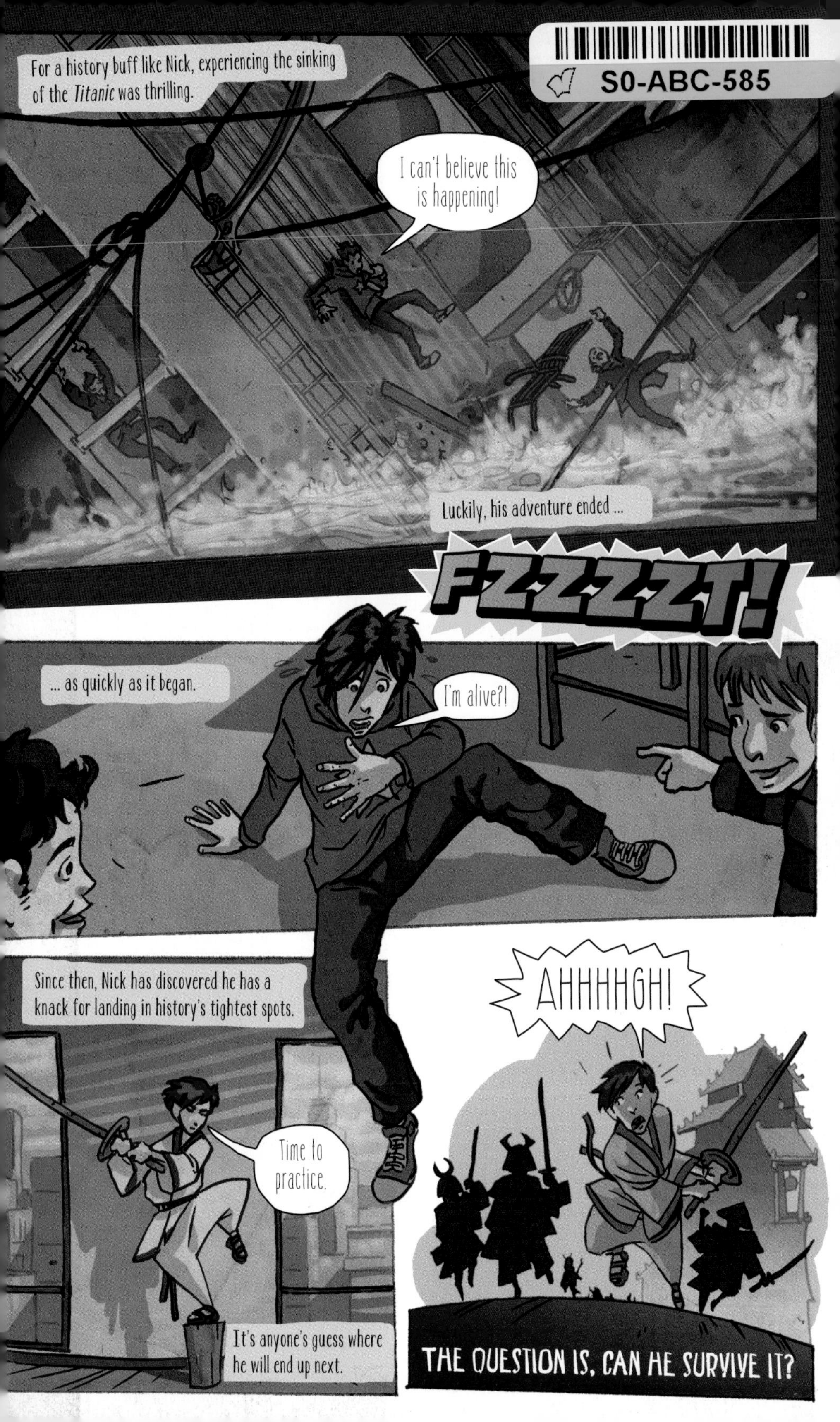

For a history buff like Nick, experiencing the sinking of the *Titanic* was thrilling.
I can't believe this is happening!
Luckily, his adventure ended ...
FZZZZT!
... as quickly as it began.
I'm alive?!
Since then, Nick has discovered he has a knack for landing in history's tightest spots.
Time to practice.
It's anyone's guess where he will end up next.
AHHHHGH!
THE QUESTION IS, CAN HE SURVIVE IT?

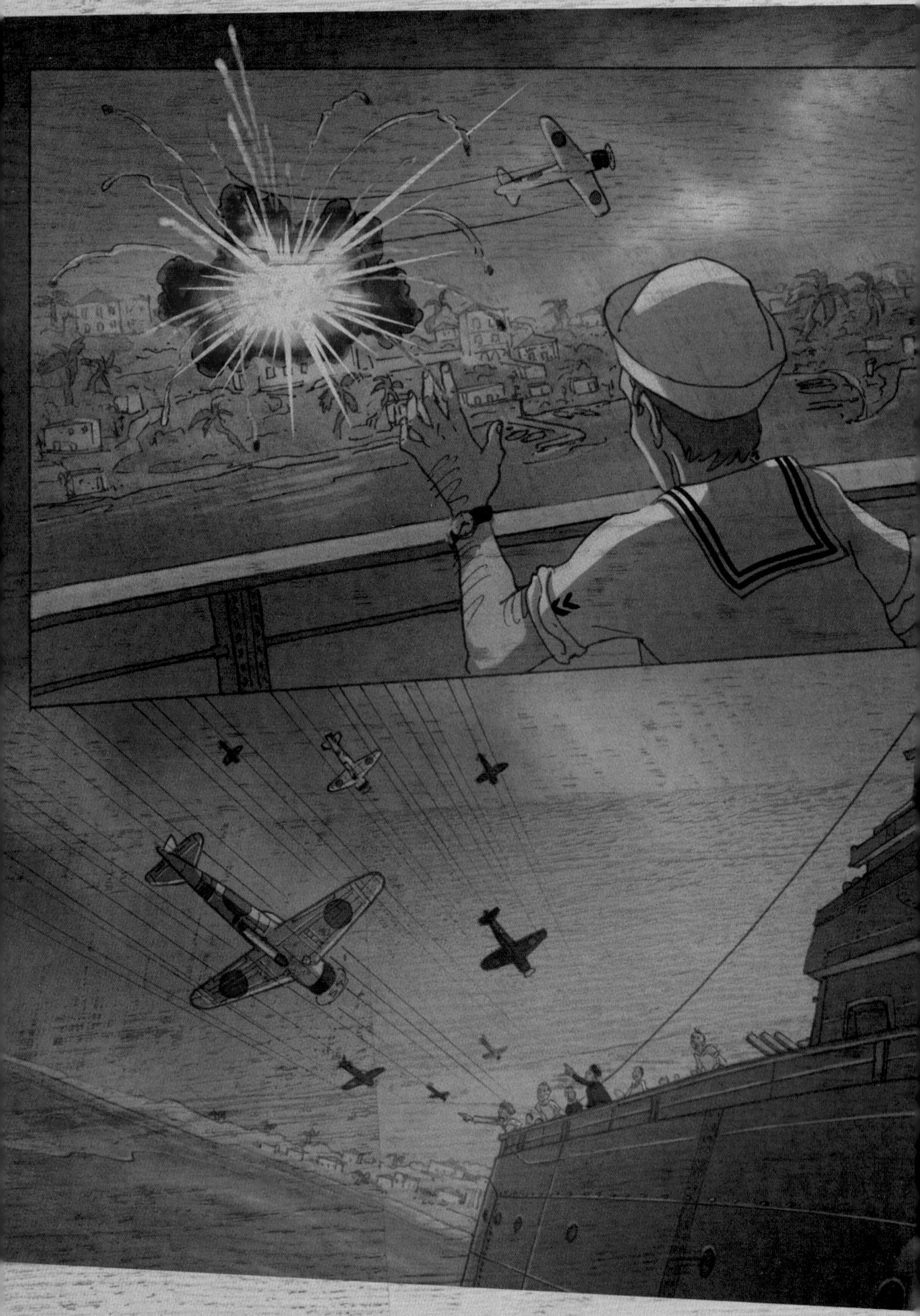

Nickolas Flux HISTORY CHRONICLES

SURPRISE ATTACK!

NICKOLAS FLUX and the Attack on Pearl Harbor

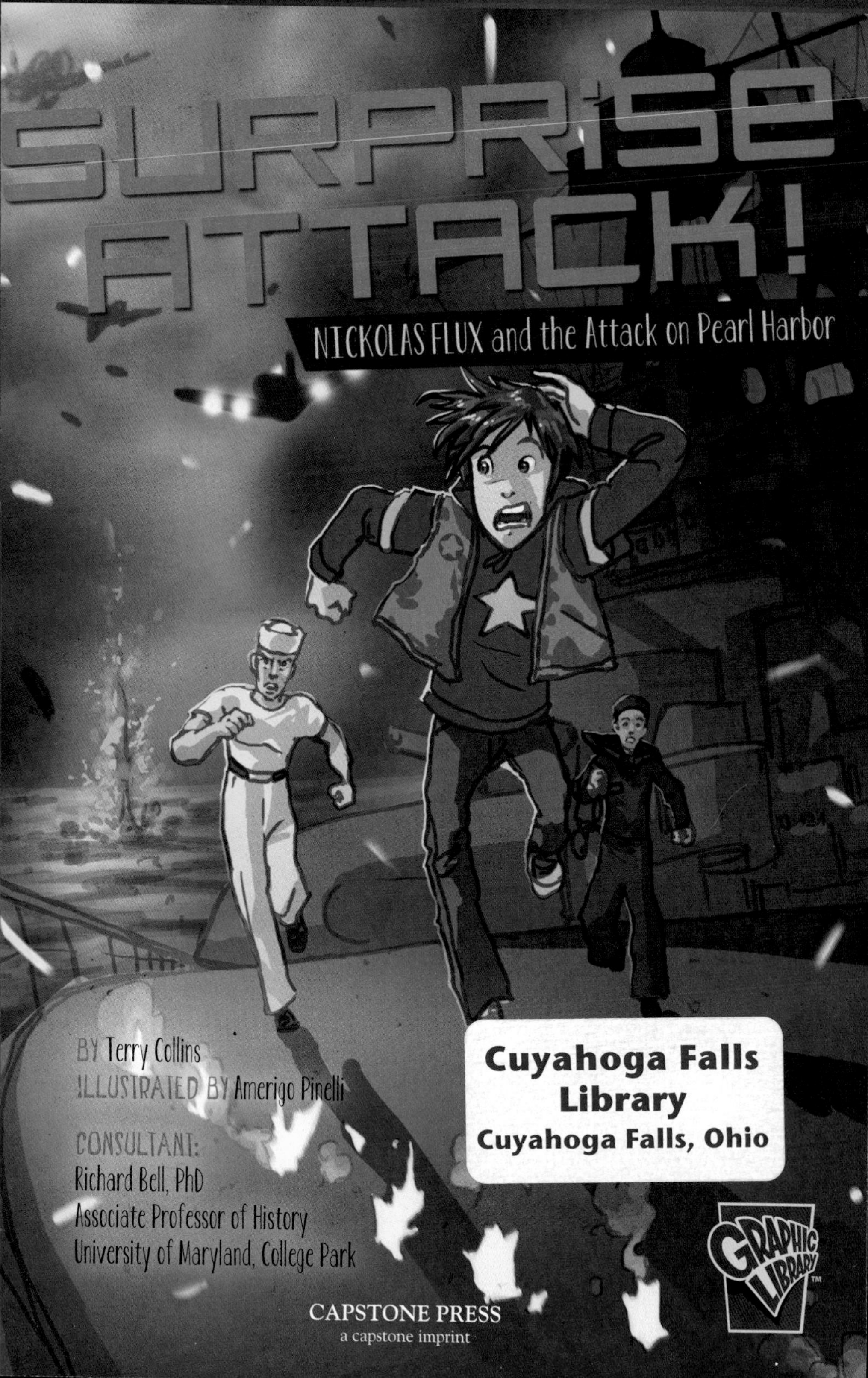

BY Terry Collins

ILLUSTRATED BY Amerigo Pinelli

CONSULTANT:
Richard Bell, PhD
Associate Professor of History
University of Maryland, College Park

CAPSTONE PRESS
a capstone imprint

Graphic Library is published by Capstone Press,
1710 Roe Crest Drive, North Mankato, Minnesota 56003
www.capstonepub.com

Library of Congress Cataloging-in-Publication Data
Collins, Terry (Terry Lee)
  Surprise attack! : Nickolas Flux and the attack on Pearl Harbor / by
Terry Collins ; illustrated by Amerigo Pinelli.
    pages cm.—(Graphic library. Nickolas Flux history chronicles)
  Includes bibliographical references and index.
  Summary: "In graphic novel format, follows the adventures of Nickolas
Flux as he travels back in time and must survive the attack on Pearl
Harbor"—Provided by publisher.
  ISBN 978-1-4914-0253-5 (library binding)
  ISBN 978-1-4914-0258-0 (paperback)
  ISBN 978-1-4914-0262-7 (eBook PDF)
1. Pearl Harbor (Hawaii), Attack on, 1941—Juvenile literature. 2.
Pearl Harbor (Hawaii), Attack on, 1941—Comic books, strips, etc. 3.
World War, 1939–1945—Causes—Juvenile literature. 4. World War,
1939–1945—Causes—Comic books, strips, etc. 5. Graphic novels. I.
Pinelli, Amerigo, illustrator. II. Title.
  D767.92.C65 2015
  940.54'26693—dc23   2014003942

Photo Credits:
Design Elements: Shutterstock (backgrounds)

EDITOR
Christopher L. Harbo

ART DIRECTOR
Nathan Gassman

DESIGNER
Ashlee Suker

PRODUCTION SPECIALIST
Jennifer Walker

COVER ARTIST
Dante Ginevra

Printed in the United States of America in Stevens Point, Wisconsin.
032014   008092WZF14

TABLE OF CONTENTS

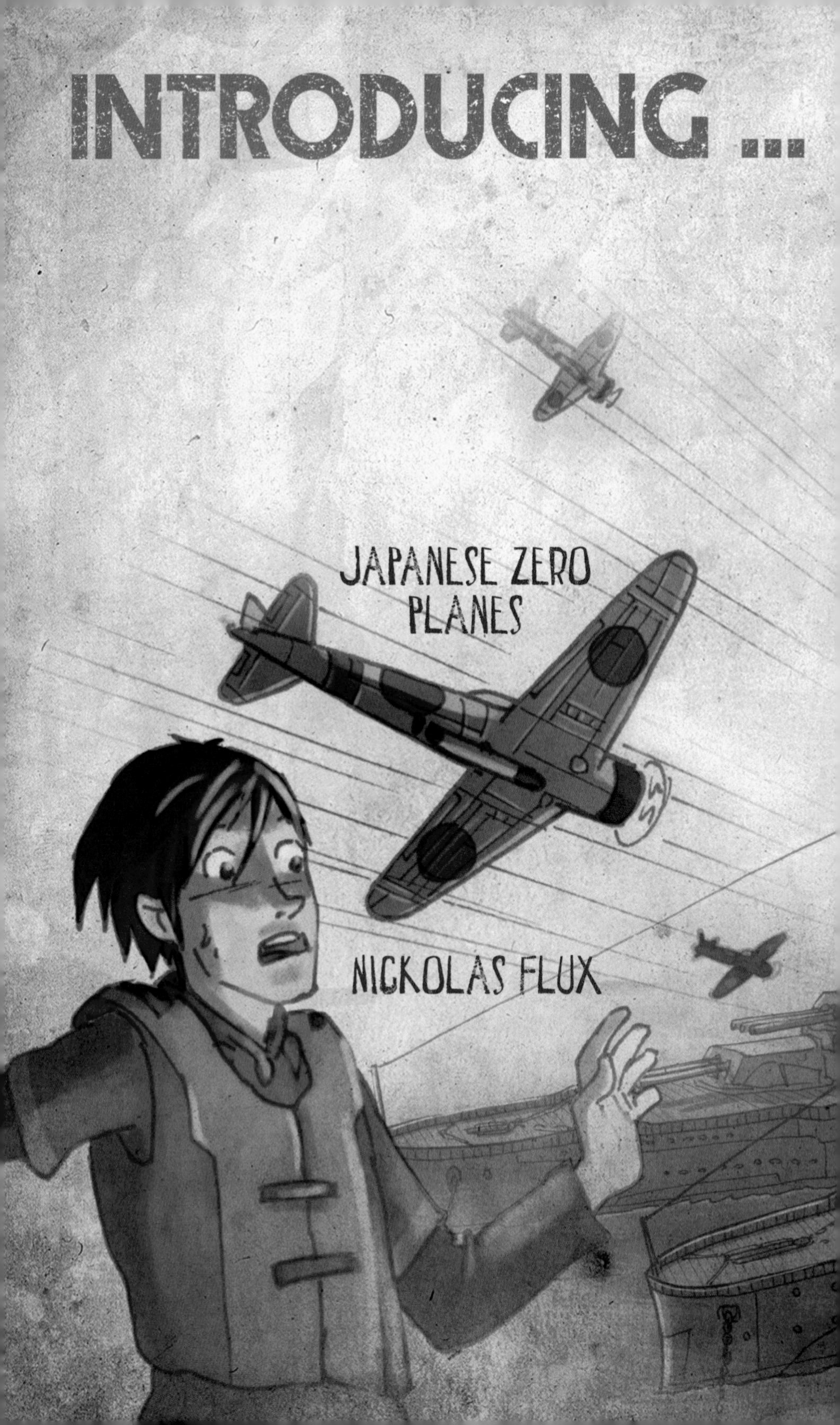
INTRODUCING ...
JAPANESE ZERO PLANES
NICKOLAS FLUX

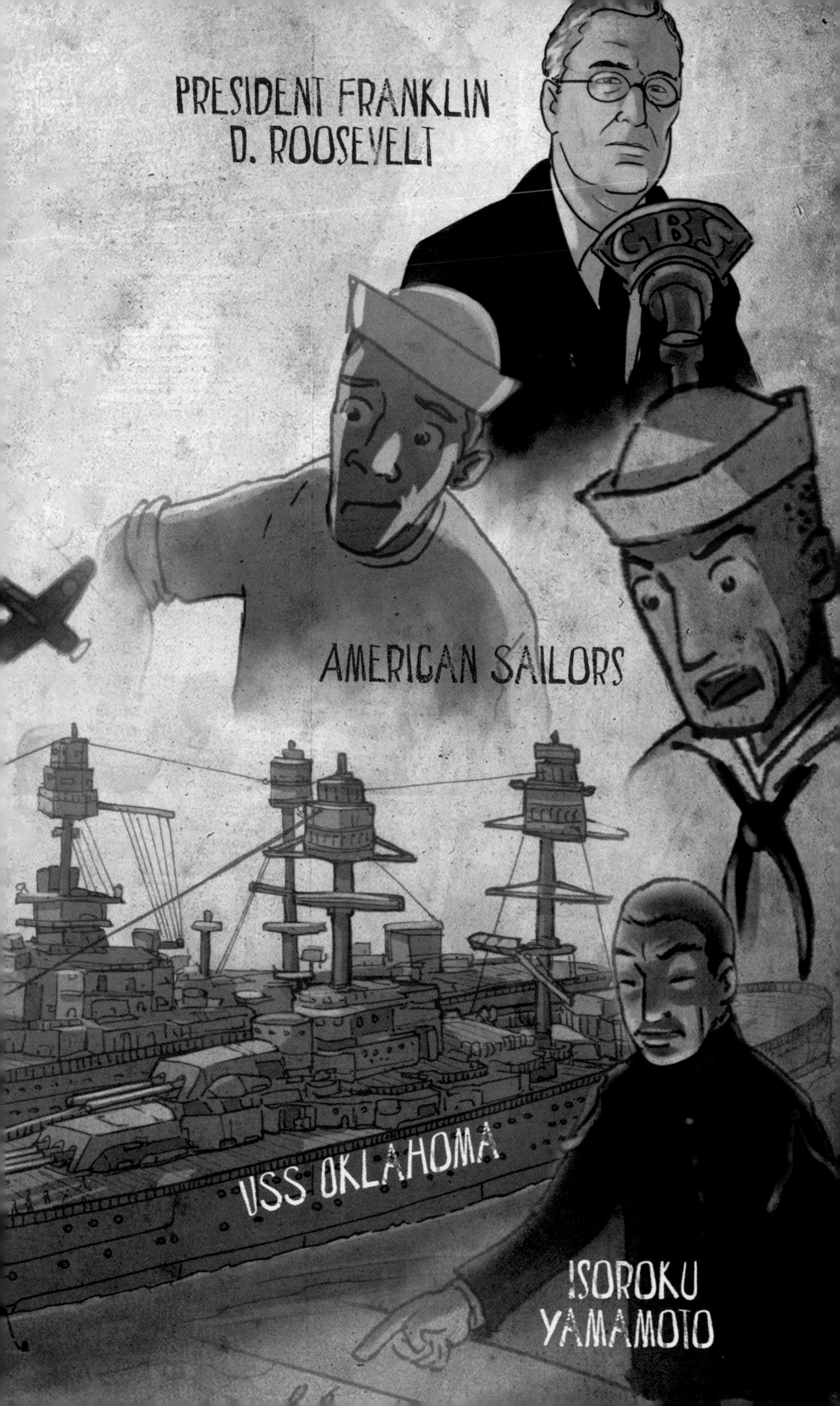

PRESIDENT FRANKLIN D. ROOSEVELT
CBS
AMERICAN SAILORS
USS OKLAHOMA
ISOROKU YAMAMOTO

CHAPTER ONE
DIVE BOMBED

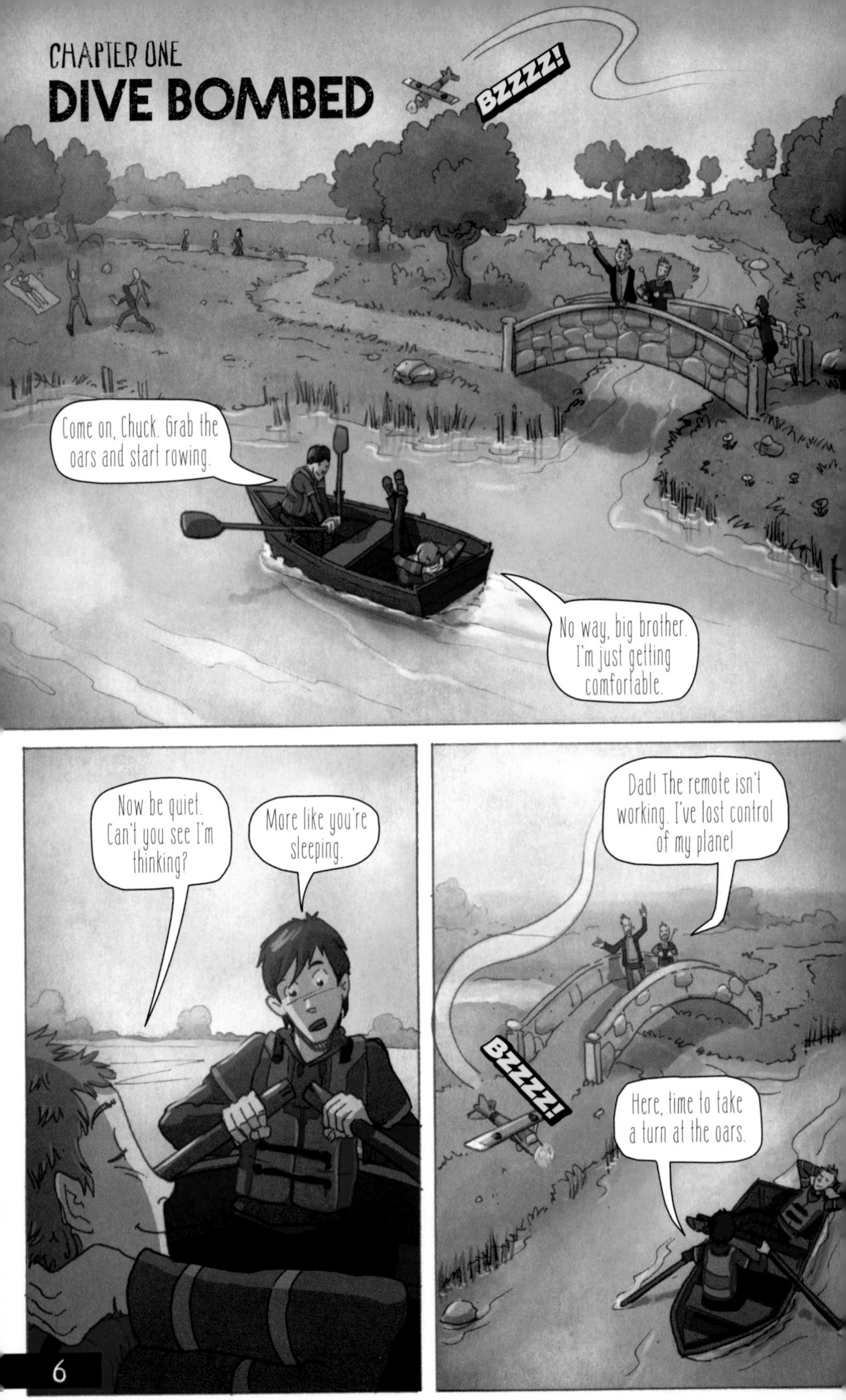
BZZZZ!
Come on, Chuck. Grab the oars and start rowing.
No way, big brother. I'm just getting comfortable.
Now be quiet. Can't you see I'm thinking?
More like you're sleeping.
Dad! The remote isn't working. I've lost control of my plane!
BZZZZ!
Here, time to take a turn at the oars.

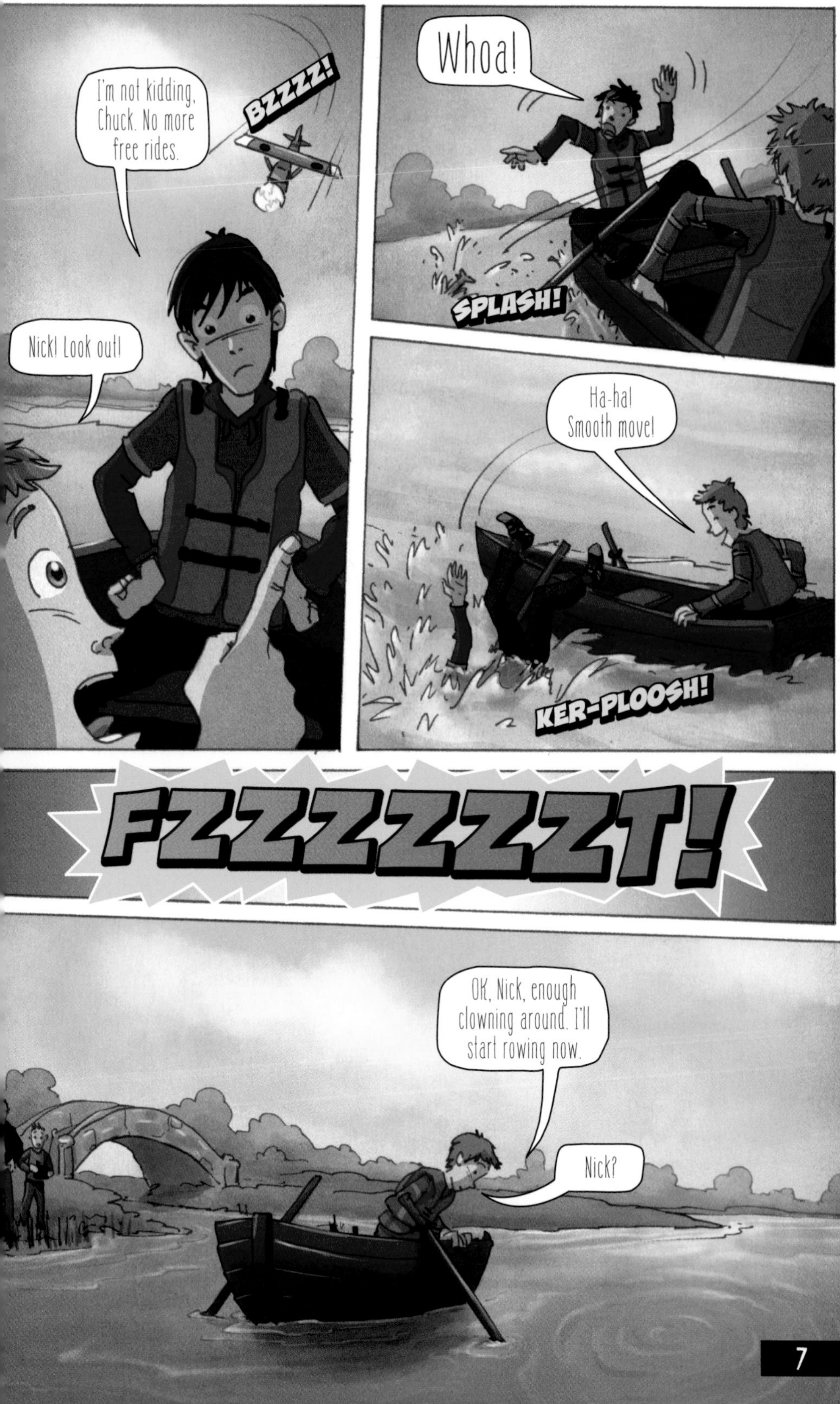

I'm not kidding, Chuck. No more free rides.
BZZZZ!
Nick! Look out!
Whoa!
SPLASH!
Ha-ha! Smooth move!
KER-PLOOSH!
FZZZZZZZT!
OK, Nick, enough clowning around. I'll start rowing now.
Nick?

CHAPTER TWO
SPLASH DOWN

Pearl Harbor, Hawaii

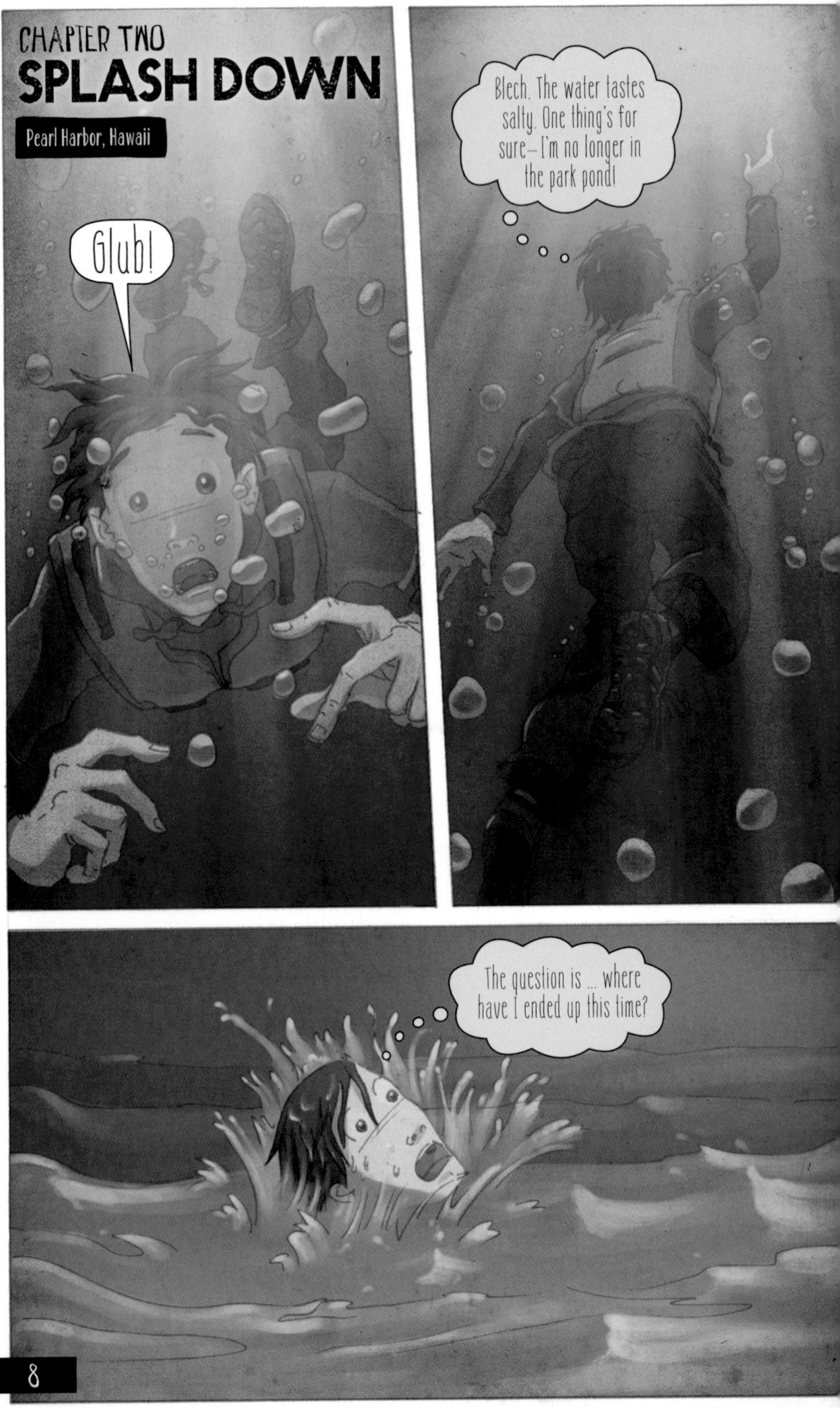
Glub!
Blech. The water tastes salty. One thing's for sure—I'm no longer in the park pond!
The question is ... where have I ended up this time?

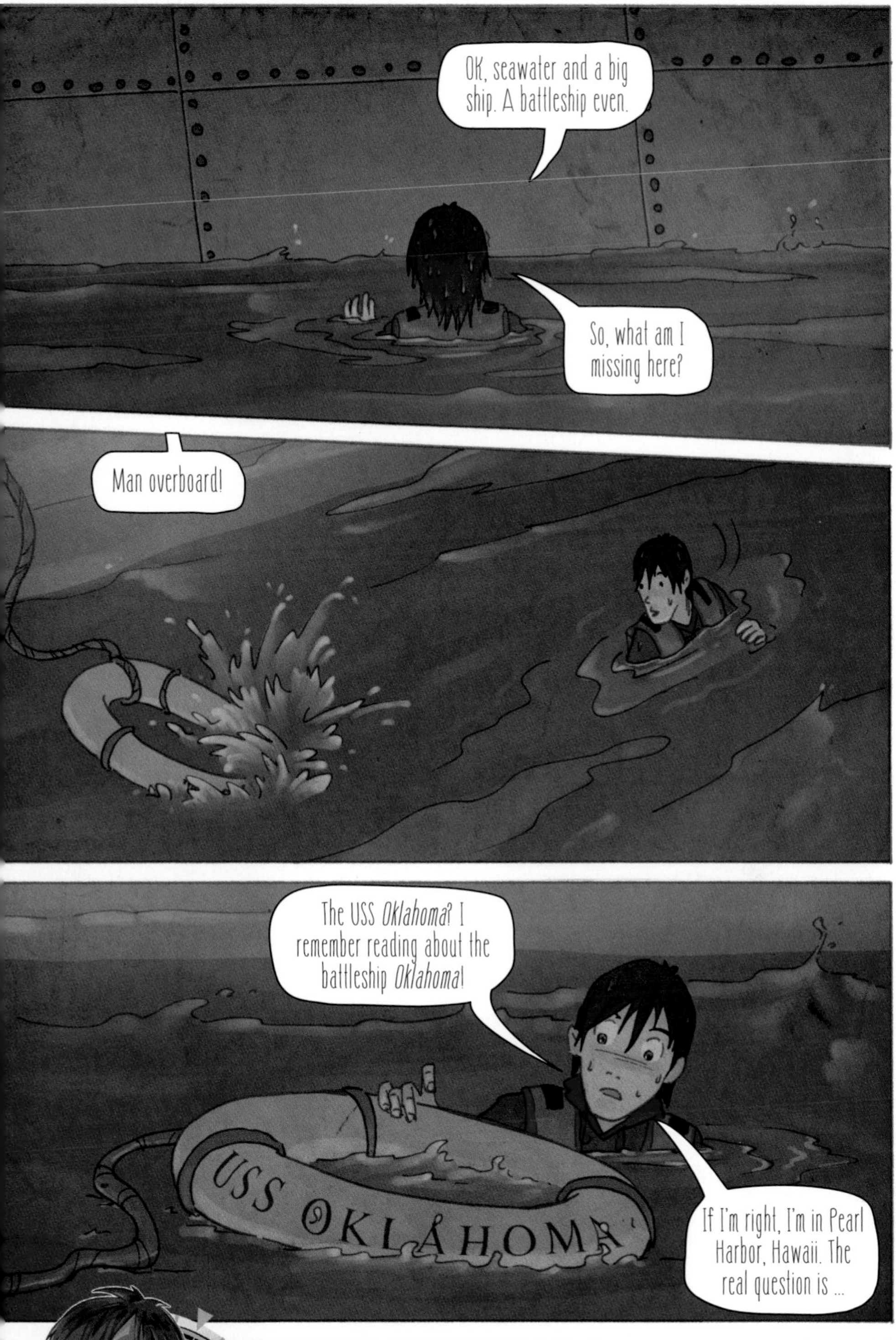
OK, seawater and a big ship. A battleship even.
So, what am I missing here?
Man overboard!
The USS *Oklahoma*? I remember reading about the battleship *Oklahoma*!
USS OKLAHOMA
If I'm right, I'm in Pearl Harbor, Hawaii. The real question is ...

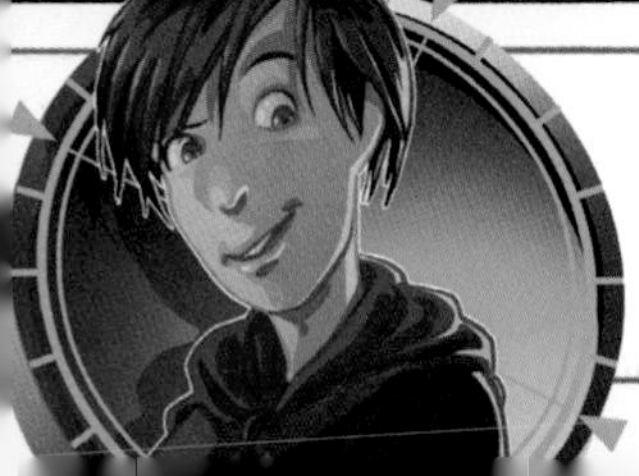

FLUX FACT

Battleships in the fleet of the United States Navy are always named after states.

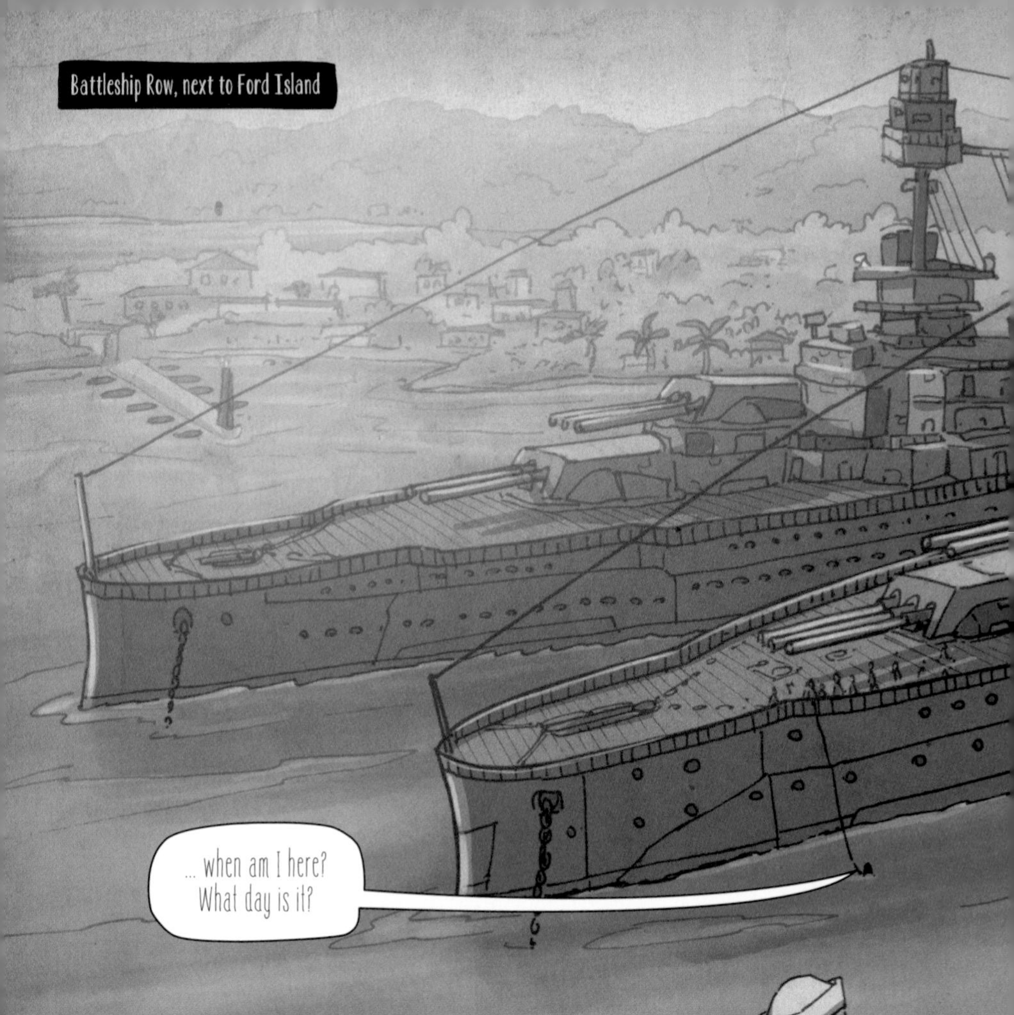
Battleship Row, next to Ford Island
... when am I here? What day is it?

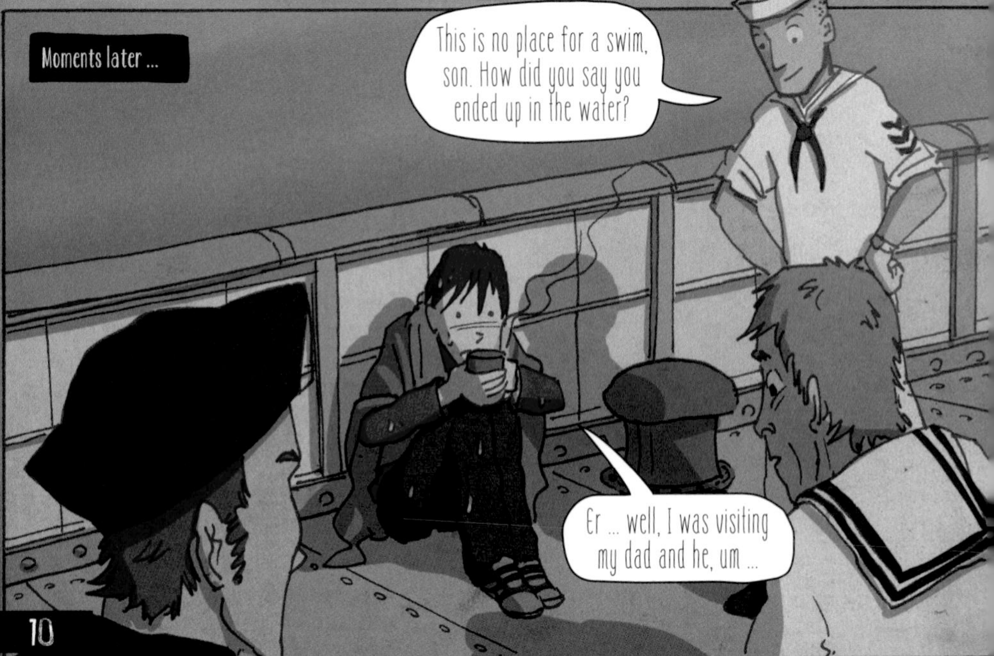
Moments later ...
This is no place for a swim, son. How did you say you ended up in the water?
Er ... well, I was visiting my dad and he, um ...

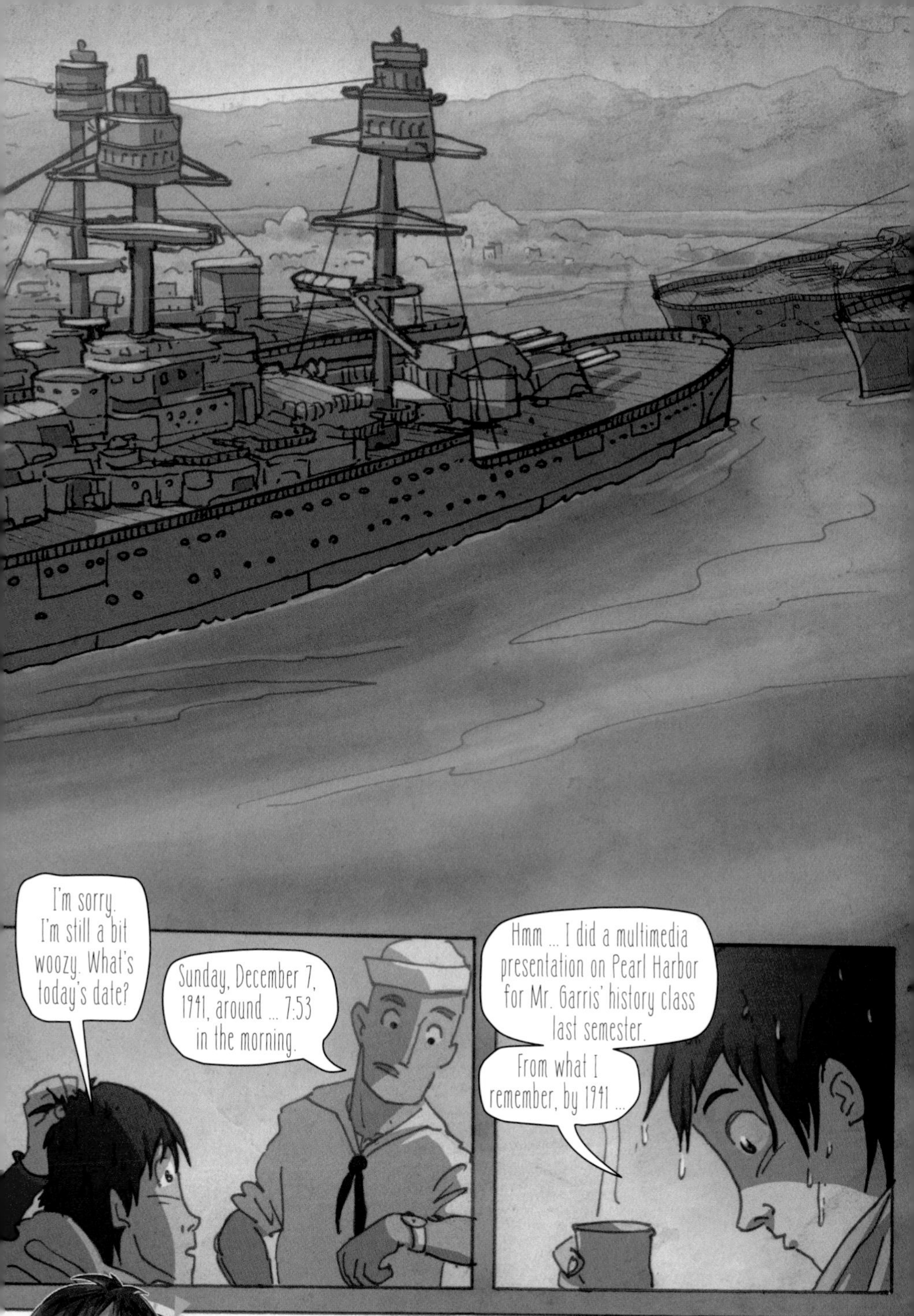
I'm sorry. I'm still a bit woozy. What's today's date?
Sunday, December 7, 1941, around ... 7:53 in the morning.
Hmm ... I did a multimedia presentation on Pearl Harbor for Mr. Garris' history class last semester.
From what I remember, by 1941 ...

FLUX FACT

Battleship Row was a group of eight United States battleships moored together next to Ford Island in Pearl Harbor. The ships were the *Arizona*, *California*, *Maryland*, *Nevada*, *Oklahoma*, *Pennsylvania*, *Tennessee*, and *West Virginia*.

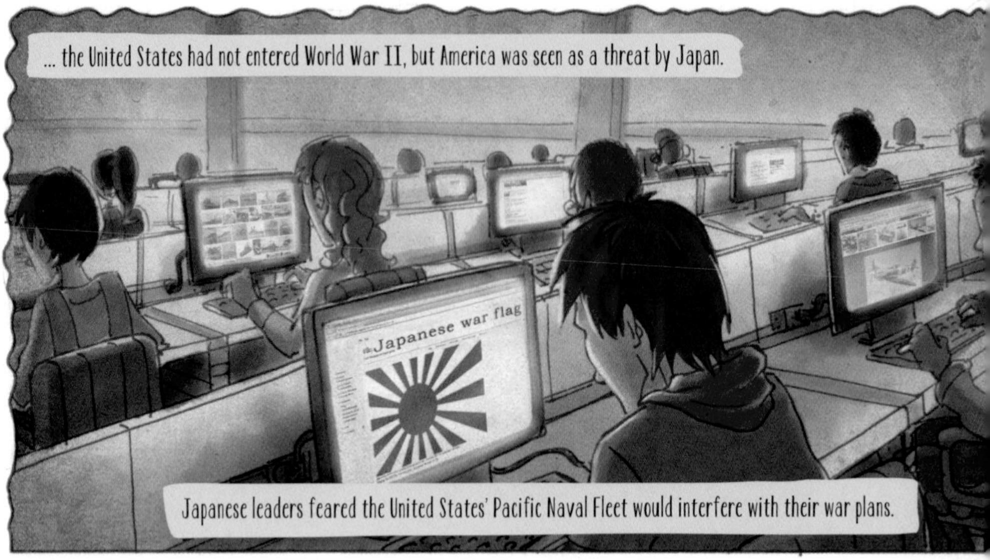
... the United States had not entered World War II, but America was seen as a threat by Japan.
Japanese war flag
Japanese leaders feared the United States' Pacific Naval Fleet would interfere with their war plans.

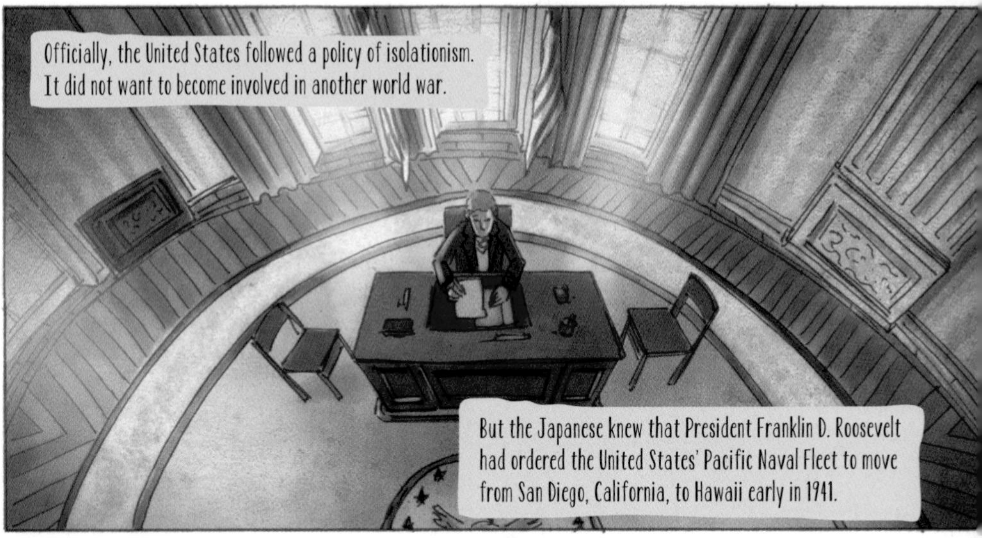
Officially, the United States followed a policy of isolationism. It did not want to become involved in another world war.
But the Japanese knew that President Franklin D. Roosevelt had ordered the United States' Pacific Naval Fleet to move from San Diego, California, to Hawaii early in 1941.

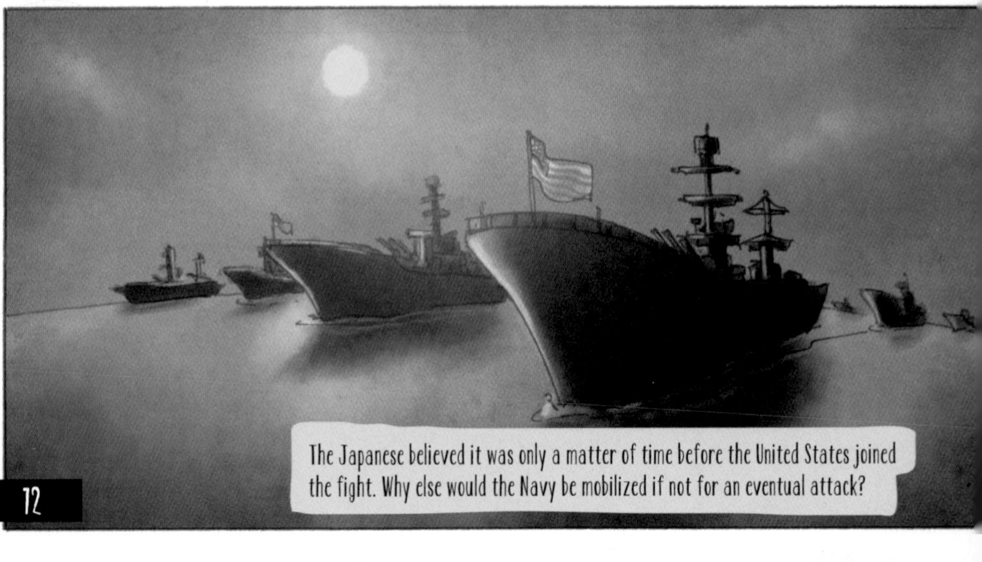
The Japanese believed it was only a matter of time before the United States joined the fight. Why else would the Navy be mobilized if not for an eventual attack?

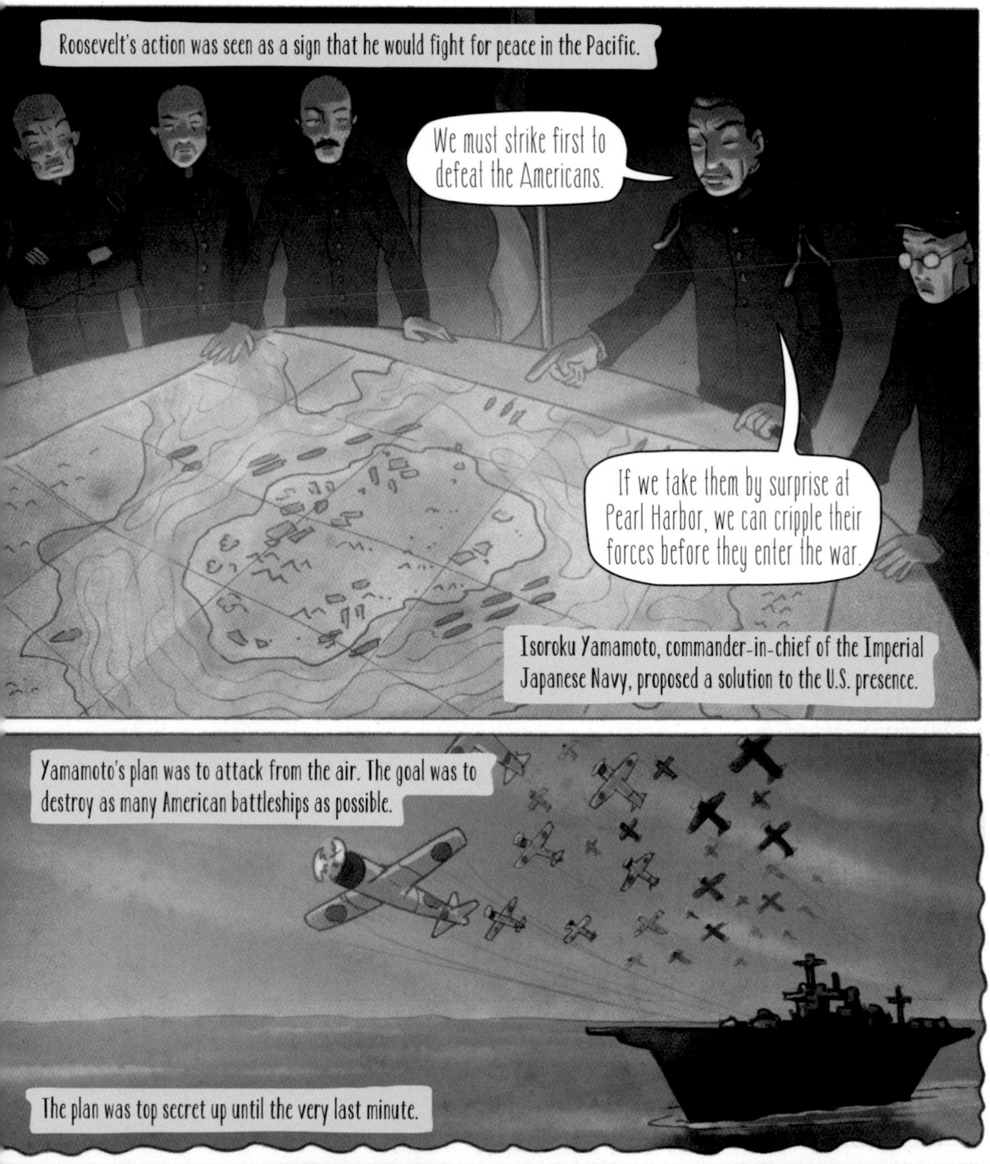
Roosevelt's action was seen as a sign that he would fight for peace in the Pacific.
We must strike first to defeat the Americans.
If we take them by surprise at Pearl Harbor, we can cripple their forces before they enter the war.
Isoroku Yamamoto, commander-in-chief of the Imperial Japanese Navy, proposed a solution to the U.S. presence.
Yamamoto's plan was to attack from the air. The goal was to destroy as many American battleships as possible.
The plan was top secret up until the very last minute.
Wait! December 7, 1941, at 7:55 a.m.?
The attack is coming right now!

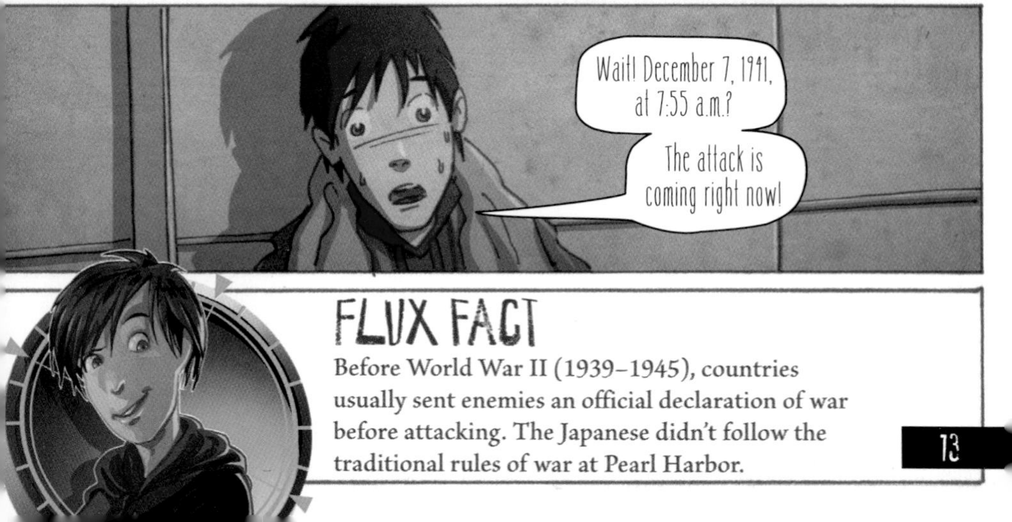

FLUX FACT

Before World War II (1939–1945), countries usually sent enemies an official declaration of war before attacking. The Japanese didn't follow the traditional rules of war at Pearl Harbor.

CHAPTER THREE

THIS IS NOT A DRILL

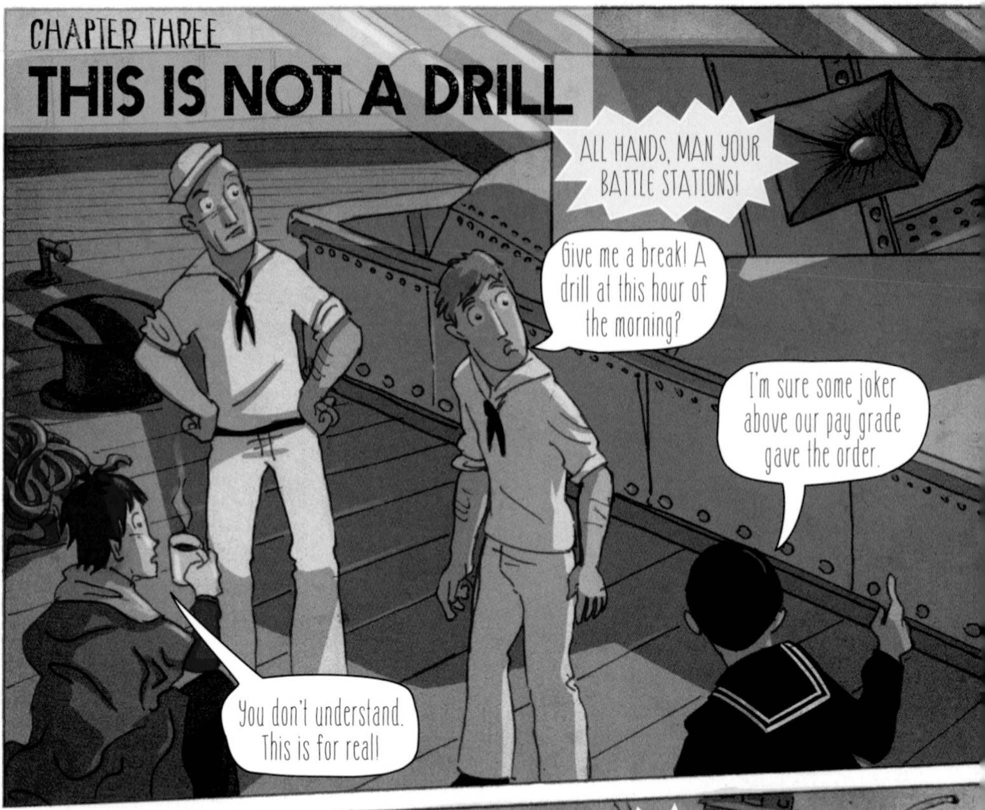

ALL HANDS, MAN YOUR BATTLE STATIONS!
Give me a break! A drill at this hour of the morning?
I'm sure some joker above our pay grade gave the order.
You don't understand. This is for real!

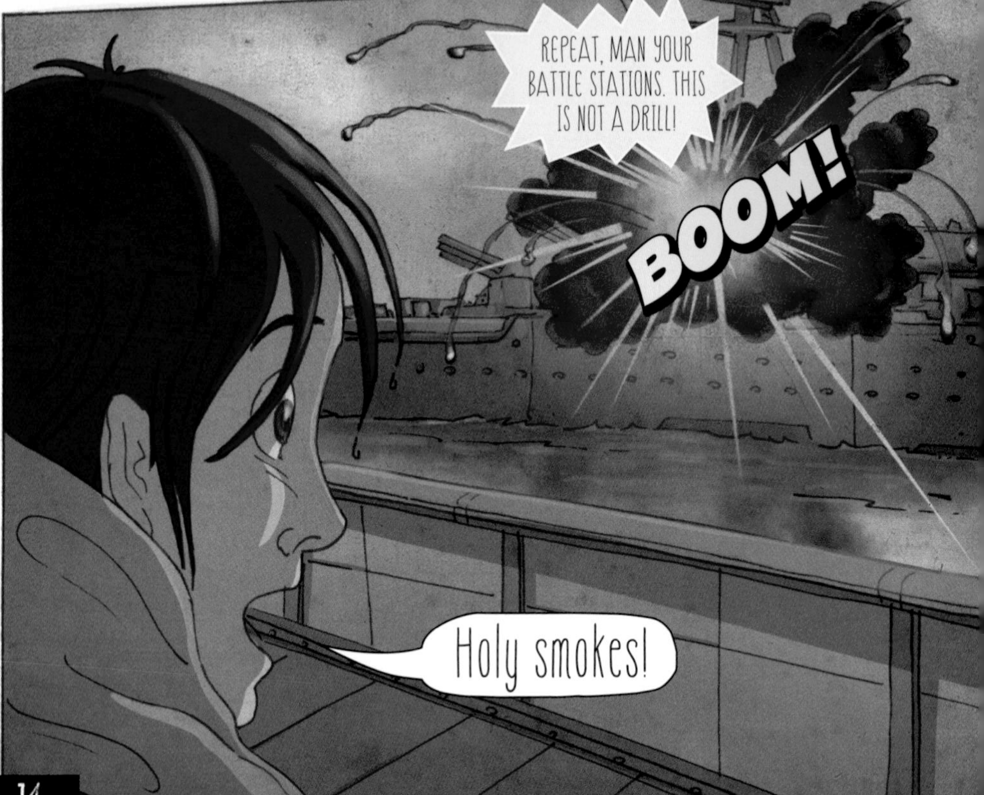

REPEAT, MAN YOUR BATTLE STATIONS. THIS IS NOT A DRILL!
BOOM!
Holy smokes!

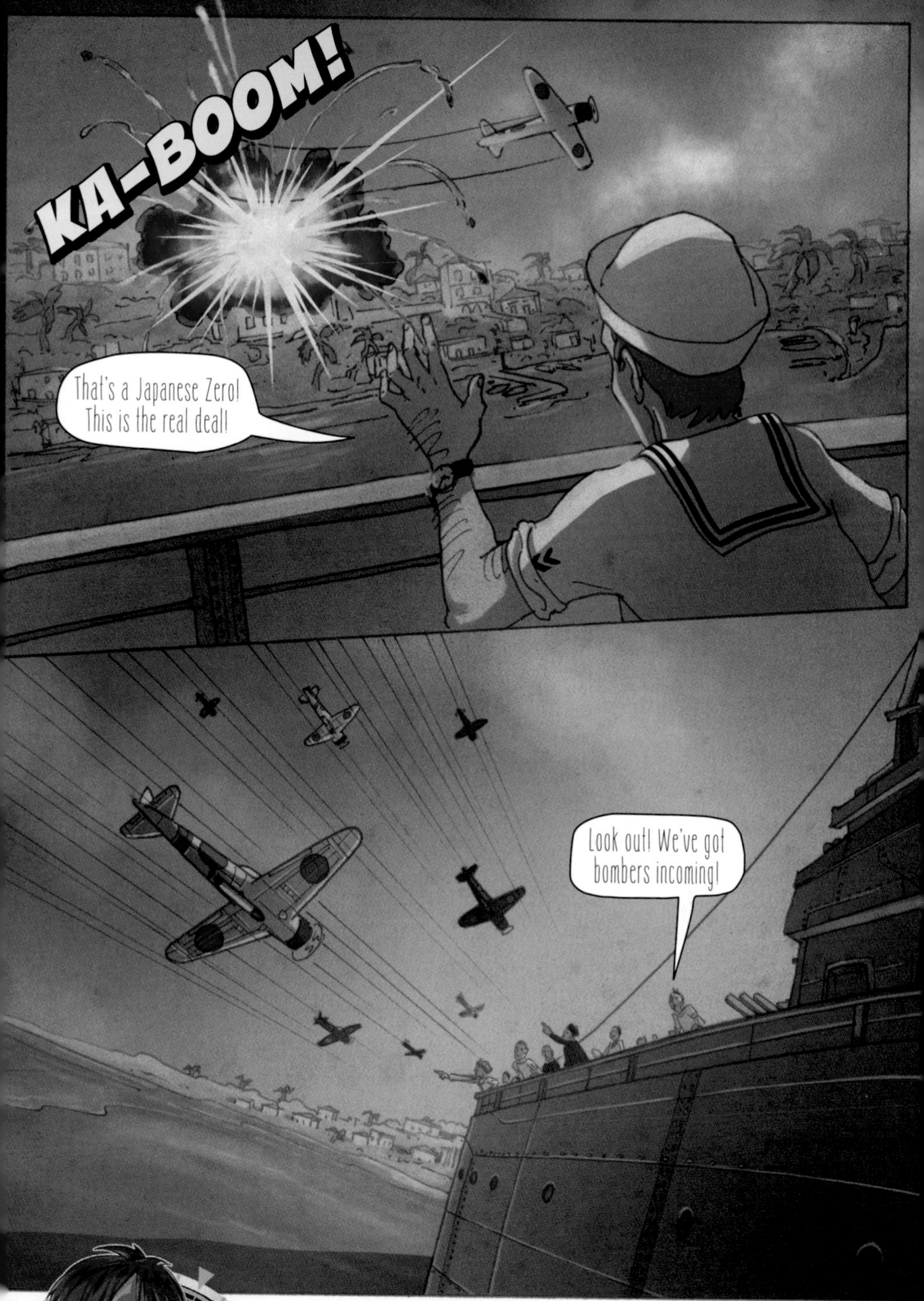
KA-BOOM!
That's a Japanese Zero! This is the real deal!
Look out! We've got bombers incoming!

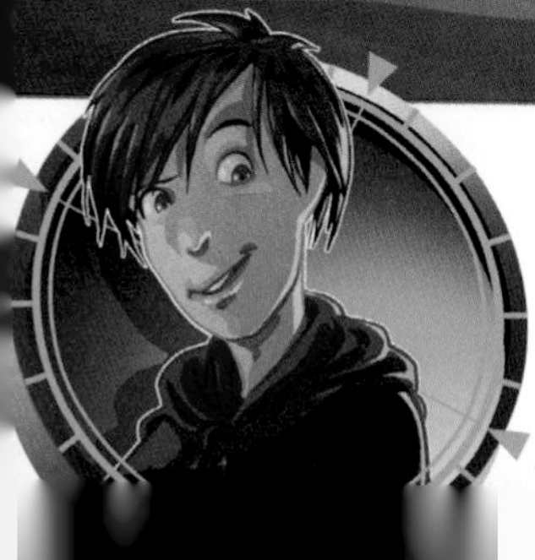

FLUX FACT

When the Japanese pilots reached their target, they radioed back "Tora, Tora, Tora" to the aircraft carriers. This phrase, meaning "Tiger, Tiger, Tiger" in English, was a code. It let the Japanese fleet commander know the surprise attack was underway.

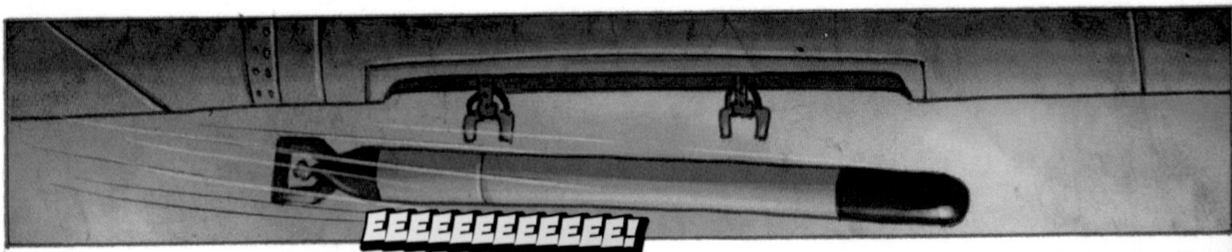
EEEEEEEEEEEE!

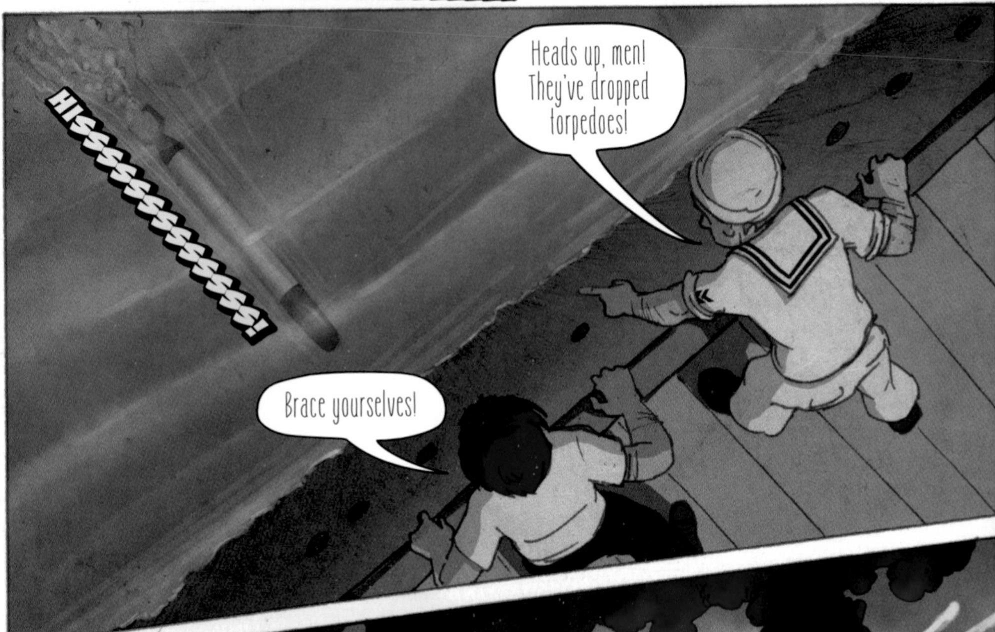
HISSSSSSSSSSSS!
Heads up, men! They've dropped torpedoes!
Brace yourselves!

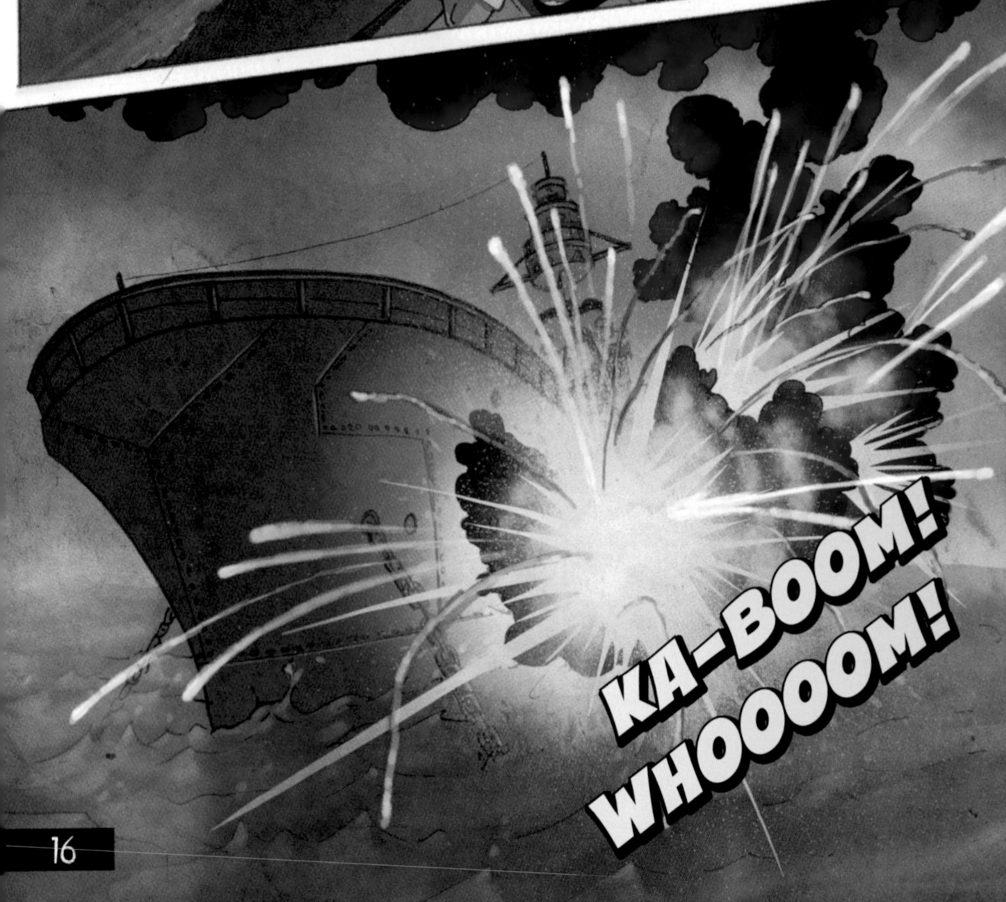
KA-BOOM!
WHOOOOM!

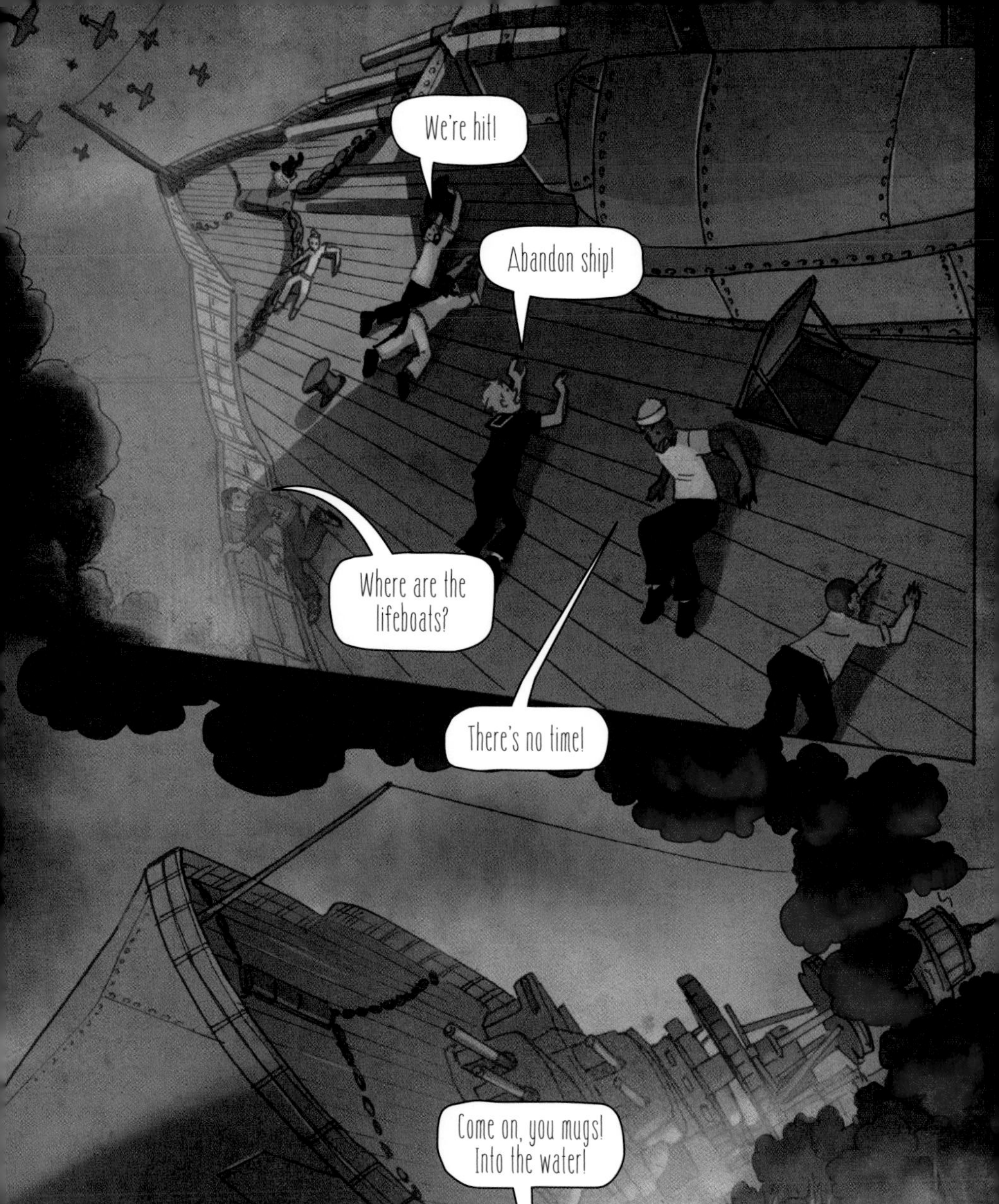

We're hit!
Abandon ship!
Where are the lifeboats?
There's no time!
Come on, you mugs! Into the water!

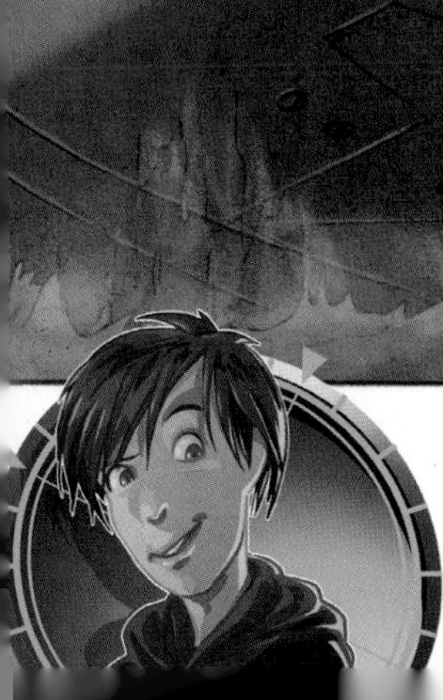

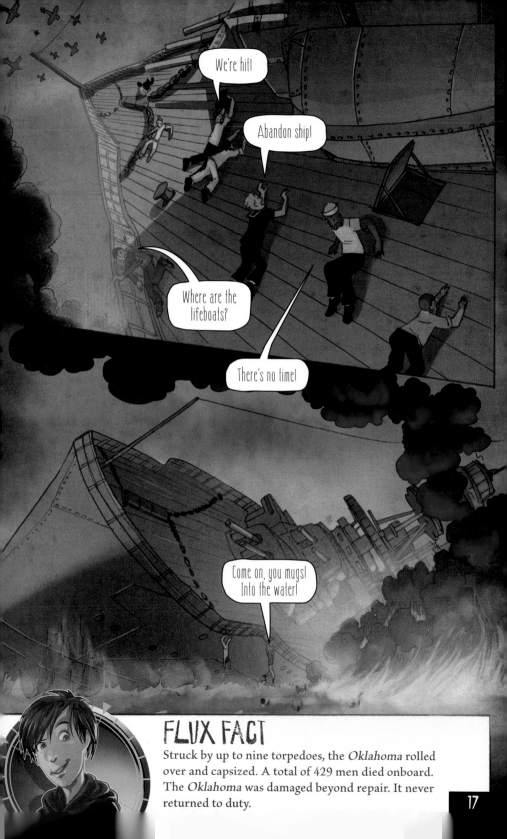

FLUX FACT

Struck by up to nine torpedoes, the *Oklahoma* rolled over and capsized. A total of 429 men died onboard. The *Oklahoma* was damaged beyond repair. It never returned to duty.

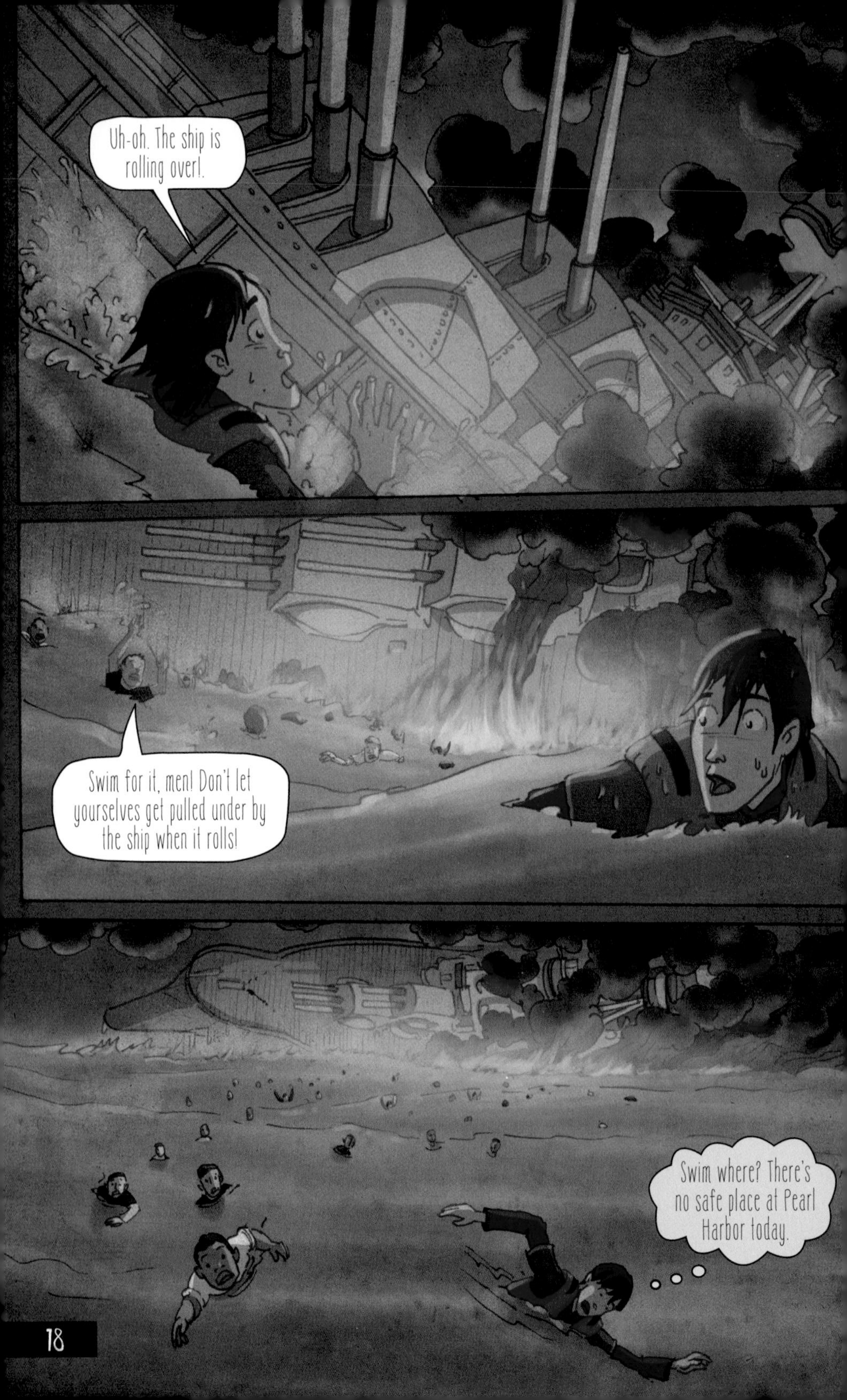
Uh-oh. The ship is rolling over!.
Swim for it, men! Don't let yourselves get pulled under by the ship when it rolls!
Swim where? There's no safe place at Pearl Harbor today.

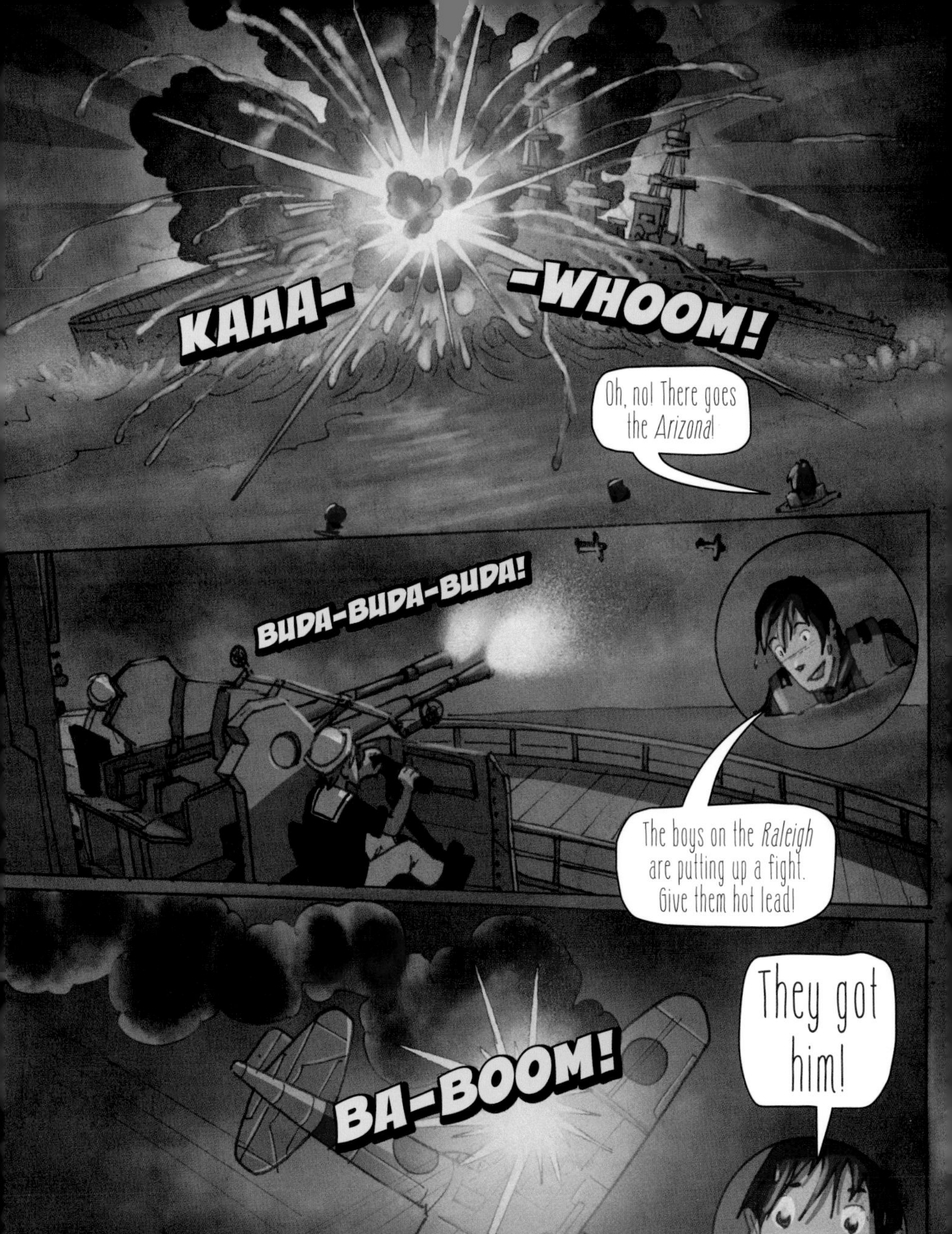
KAAA-
-WHOOM!
Oh, no! There goes the *Arizona*!
BUDA-BUDA-BUDA!
The boys on the *Raleigh* are putting up a fight. Give them hot lead!
BA-BOOM!
They got him!

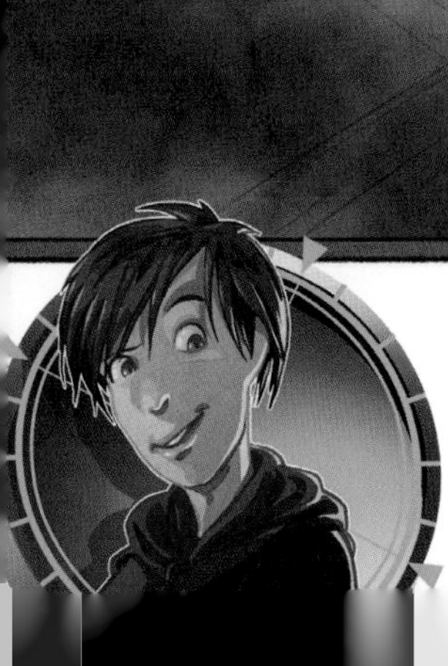

FLUX FACT

The USS *Arizona* was hit by several bombs. The last one delivered the death blow. It struck the ship's ammunition magazine, causing a massive explosion. The ship quickly settled on the bottom of the harbor. A total of 1,177 crewmen went down with the ship.

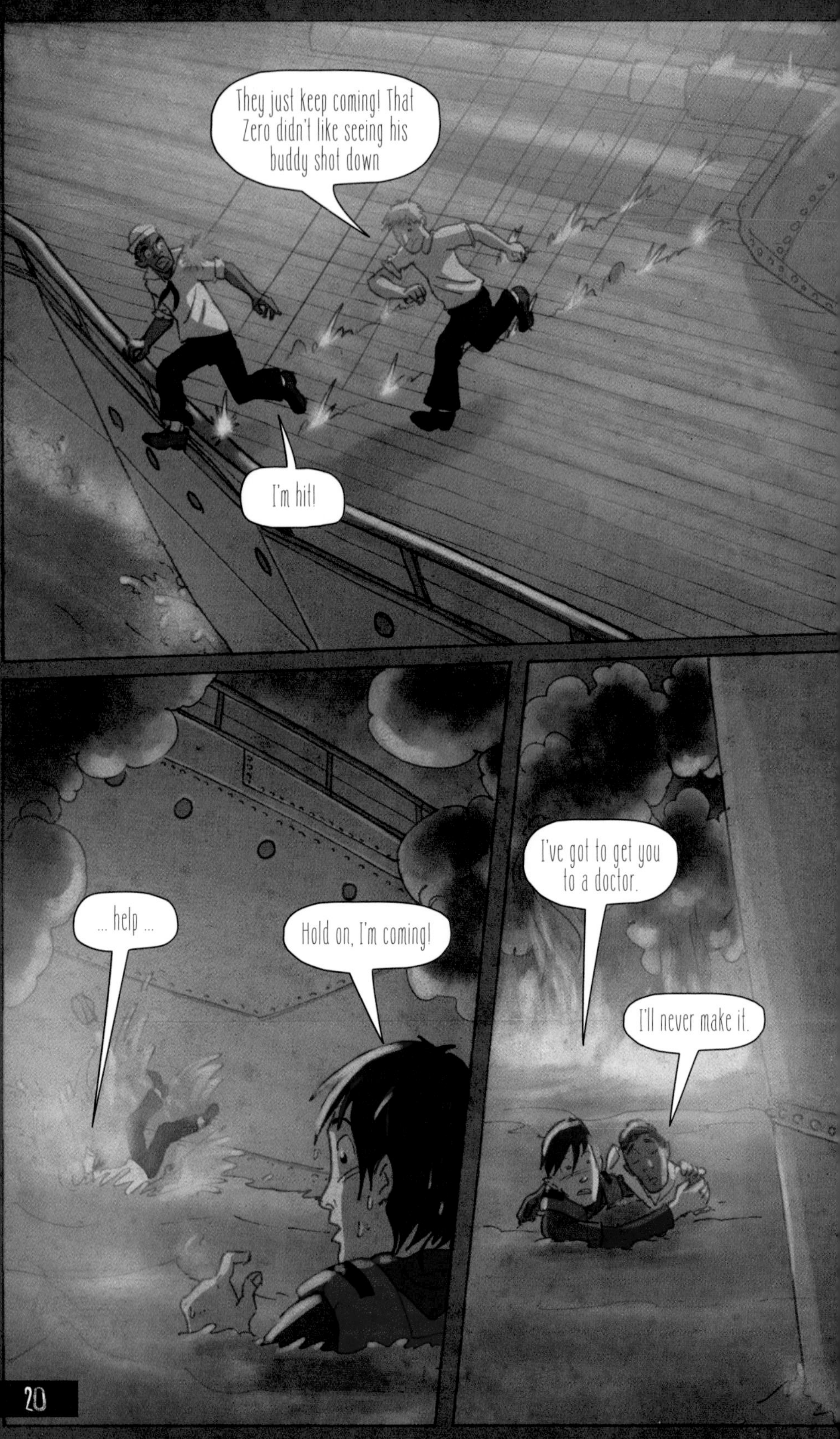
They just keep coming! That Zero didn't like seeing his buddy shot down
I'm hit!
... help ...
Hold on, I'm coming!
I've got to get you to a doctor.
I'll never make it.

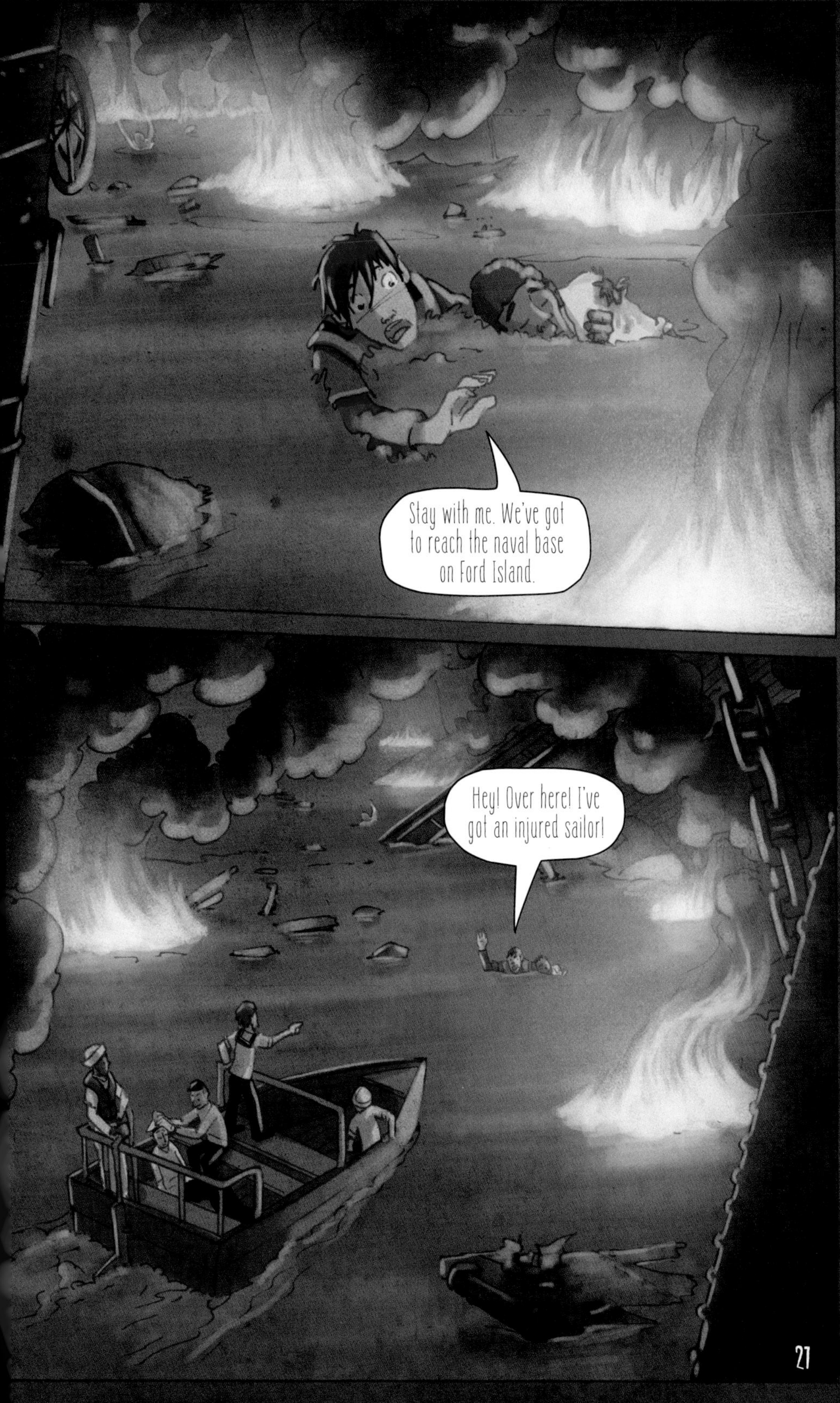
Stay with me. We've got to reach the naval base on Ford Island.
Hey! Over here! I've got an injured sailor!

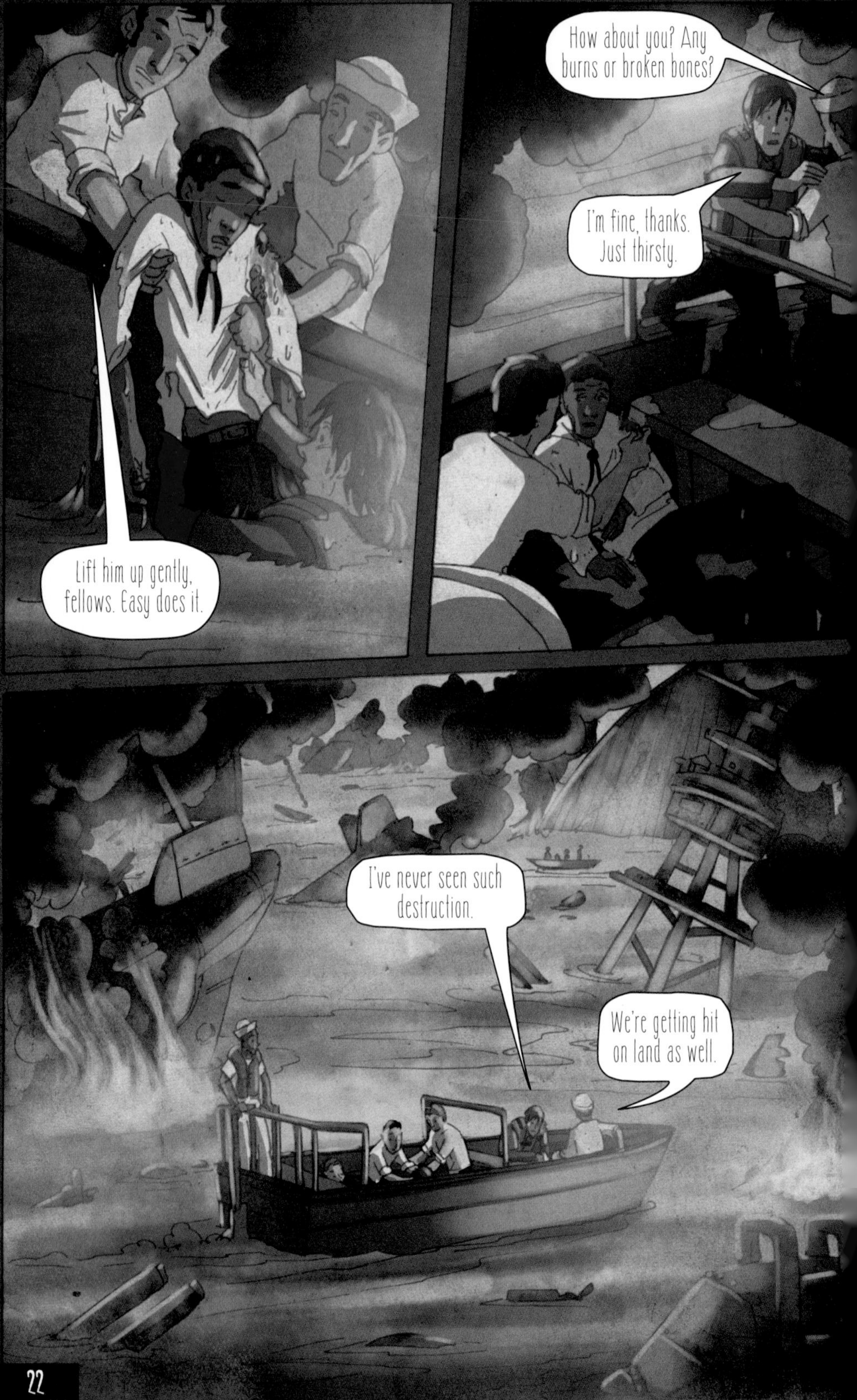
Lift him up gently, fellows. Easy does it.
How about you? Any burns or broken bones?
I'm fine, thanks. Just thirsty.
I've never seen such destruction.
We're getting hit on land as well.

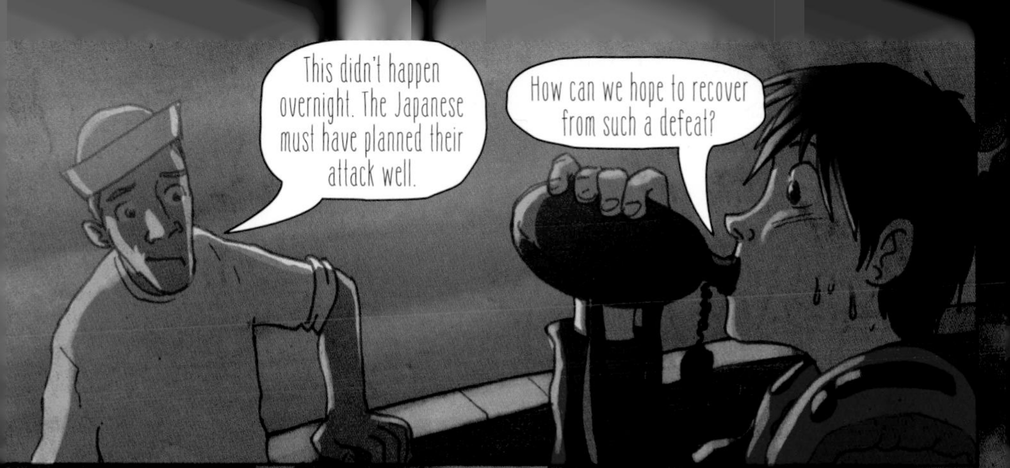
This didn't happen overnight. The Japanese must have planned their attack well.
How can we hope to recover from such a defeat?

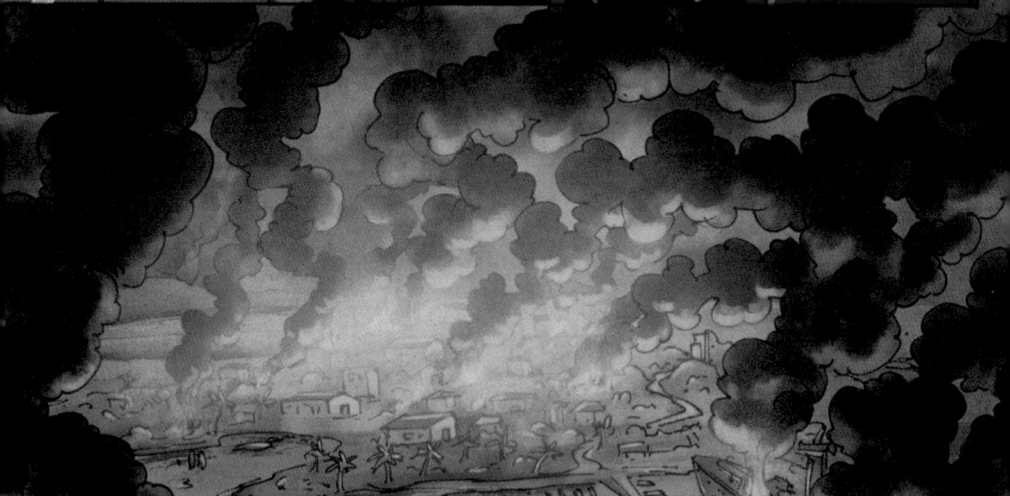
This fight isn't over yet, kid. Not by a long shot.
But first we've got to take care of our wounded.

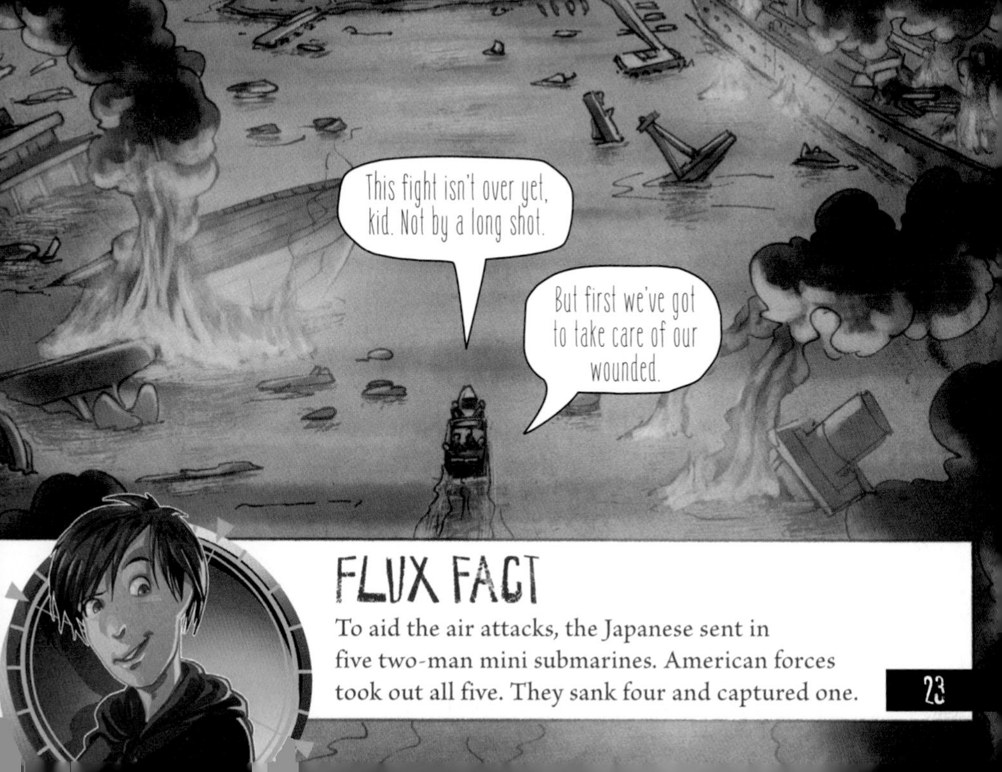

FLUX FACT

To aid the air attacks, the Japanese sent in five two-man mini submarines. American forces took out all five. They sank four and captured one.

CHAPTER FOUR
A DAY OF INFAMY

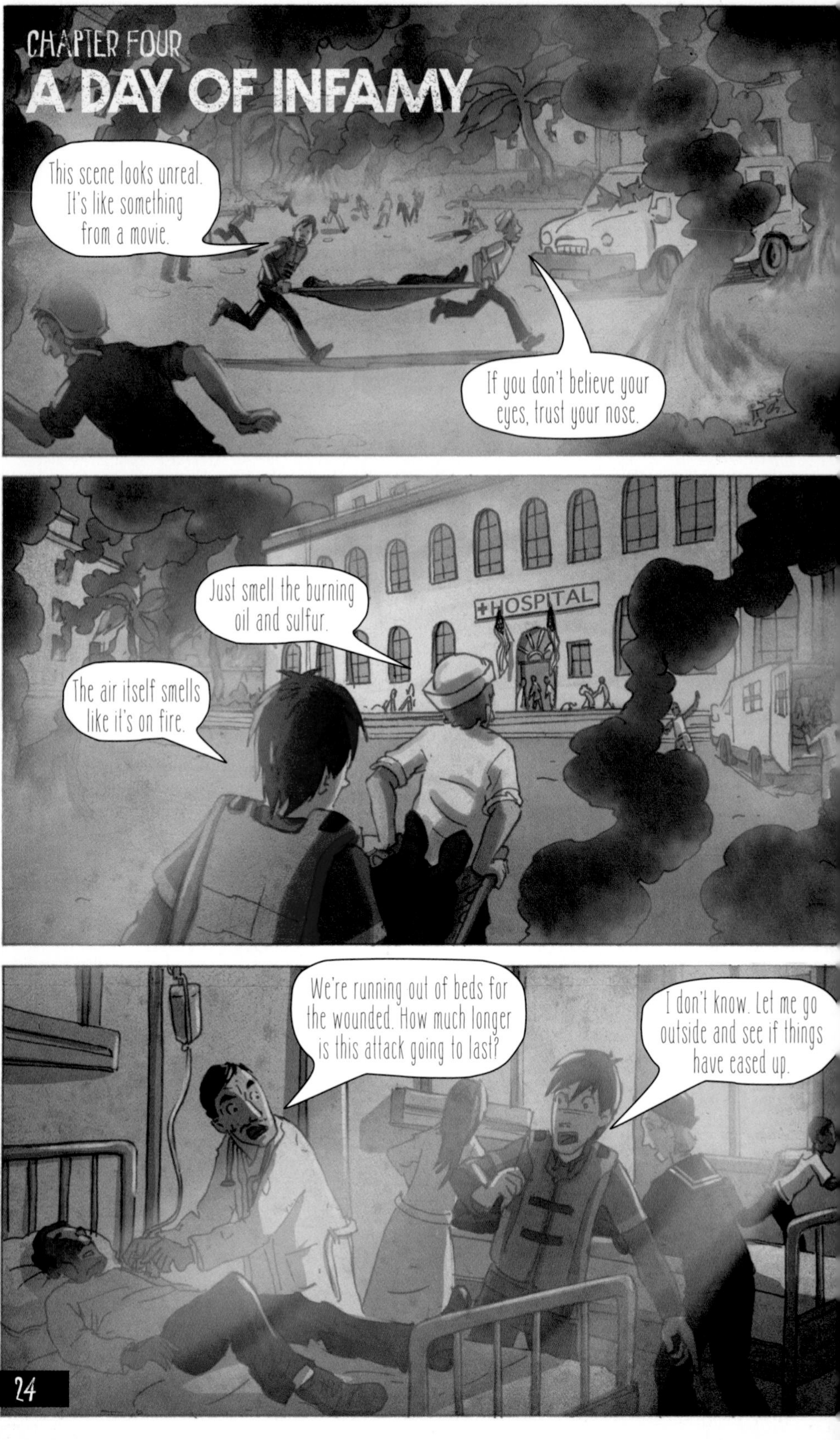
This scene looks unreal. It's like something from a movie.
If you don't believe your eyes, trust your nose.
+HOSPITAL
Just smell the burning oil and sulfur.
The air itself smells like it's on fire.
We're running out of beds for the wounded. How much longer is this attack going to last?
I don't know. Let me go outside and see if things have eased up.

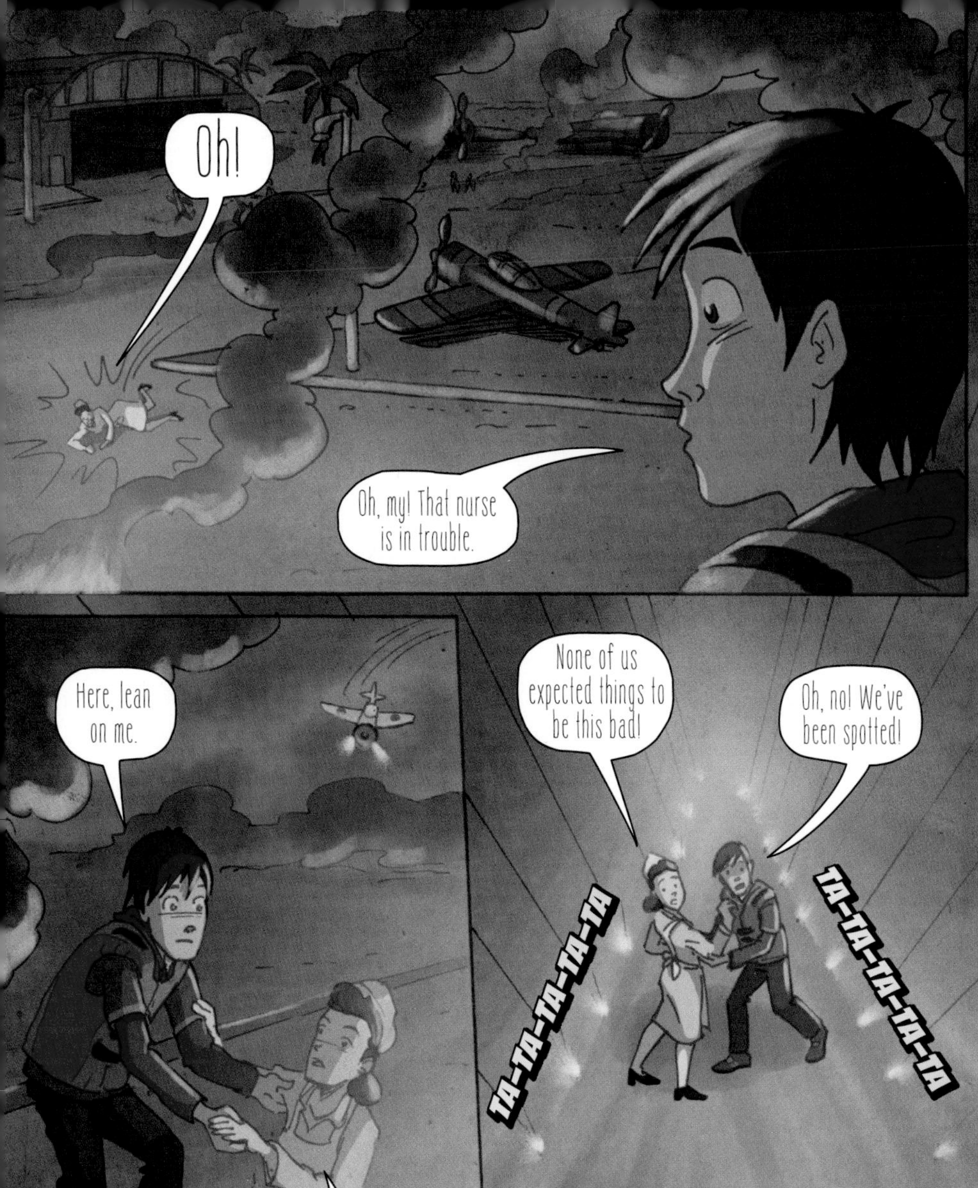

Oh!
Oh, my! That nurse is in trouble.
Here, lean on me.
Thank you. Some of us heard the air raid sirens from the hospital and came to see if there was anything we could do.
None of us expected things to be this bad!
Oh, no! We've been spotted!
TA-TA-TA-TA-TA
TA-TA-TA-TA-TA-TA

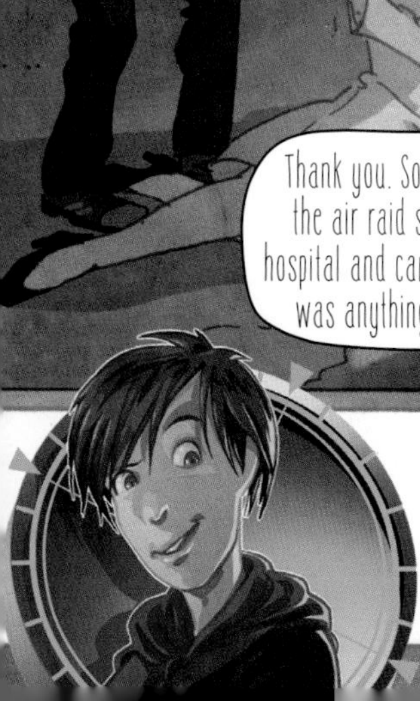

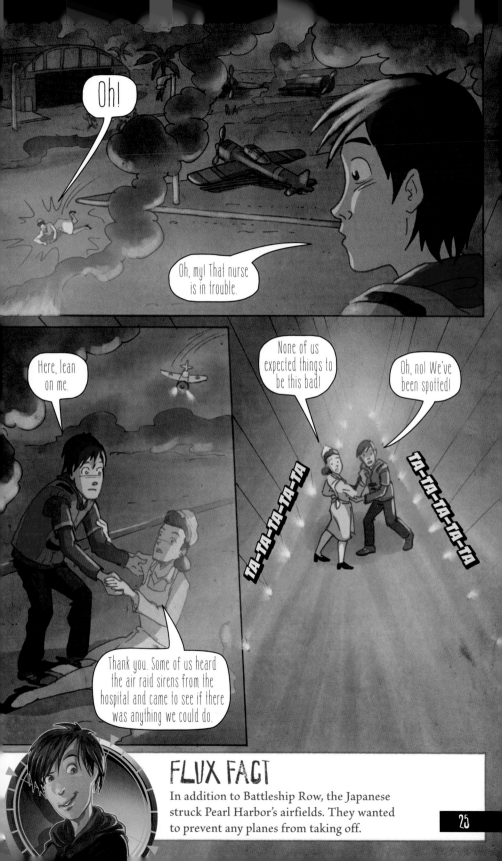

FLUX FACT

In addition to Battleship Row, the Japanese struck Pearl Harbor's airfields. They wanted to prevent any planes from taking off.

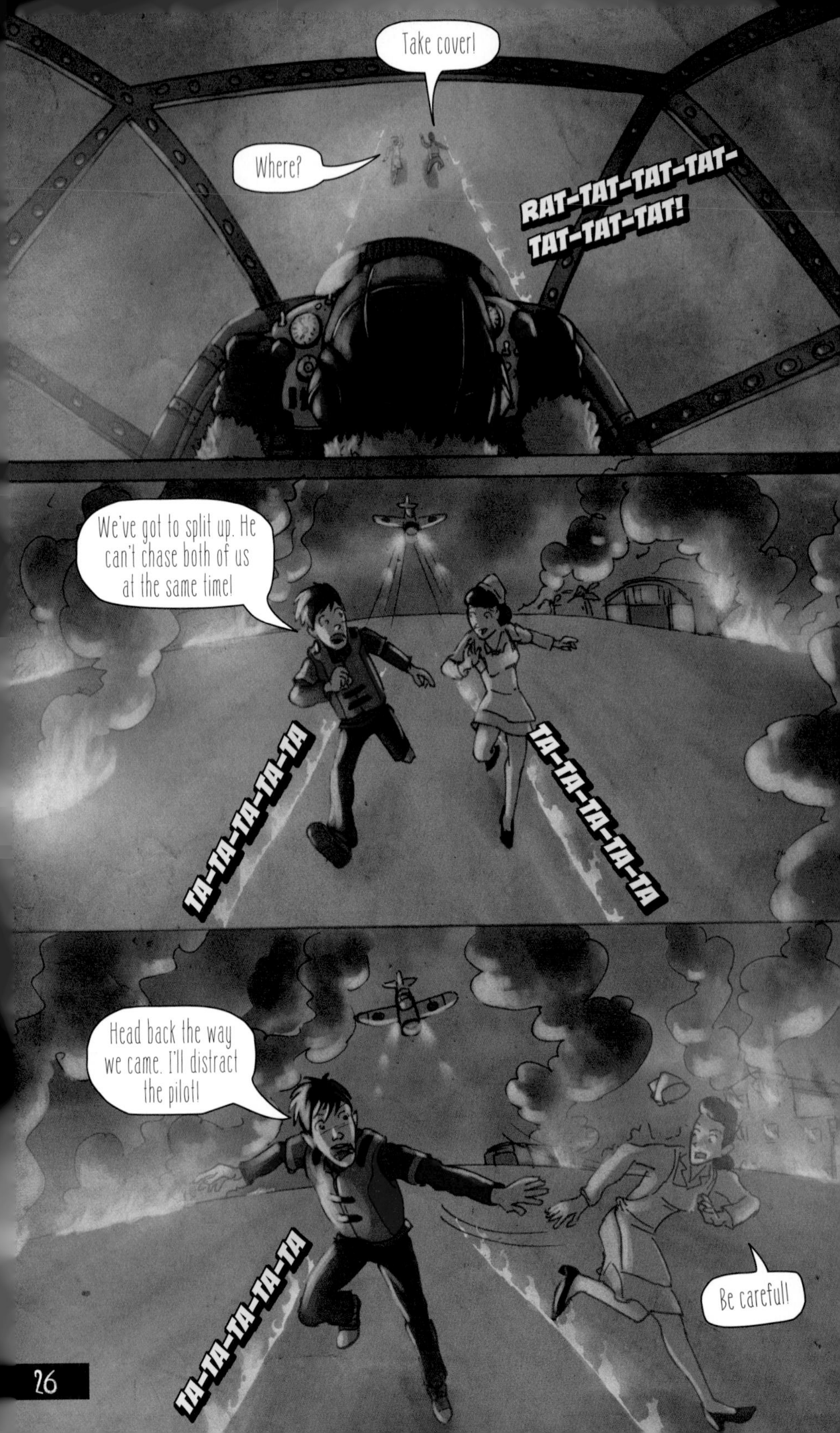

Take cover!
Where?
RAT-TAT-TAT-TAT-TAT-TAT-TAT!
We've got to split up. He can't chase both of us at the same time!
TA-TA-TA-TA-TA-TA
TA-TA-TA-TA-TA-TA
Head back the way we came. I'll distract the pilot!
TA-TA-TA-TA-TA-TA
Be careful!

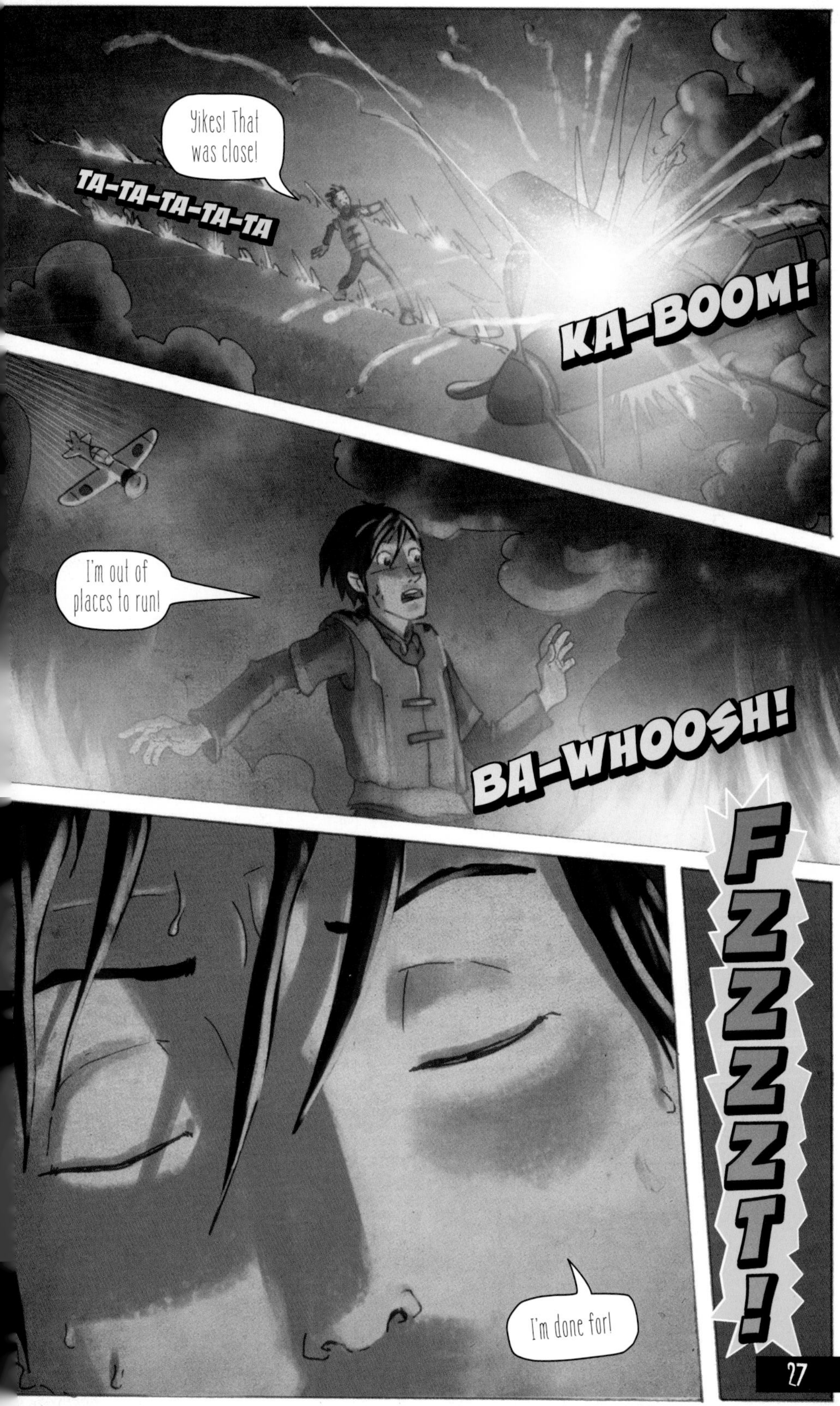

Yikes! That was close!
TA-TA-TA-TA-TA
KA-BOOM!
I'm out of places to run!
BA-WHOOSH!
FZZZZZT!
I'm done for!

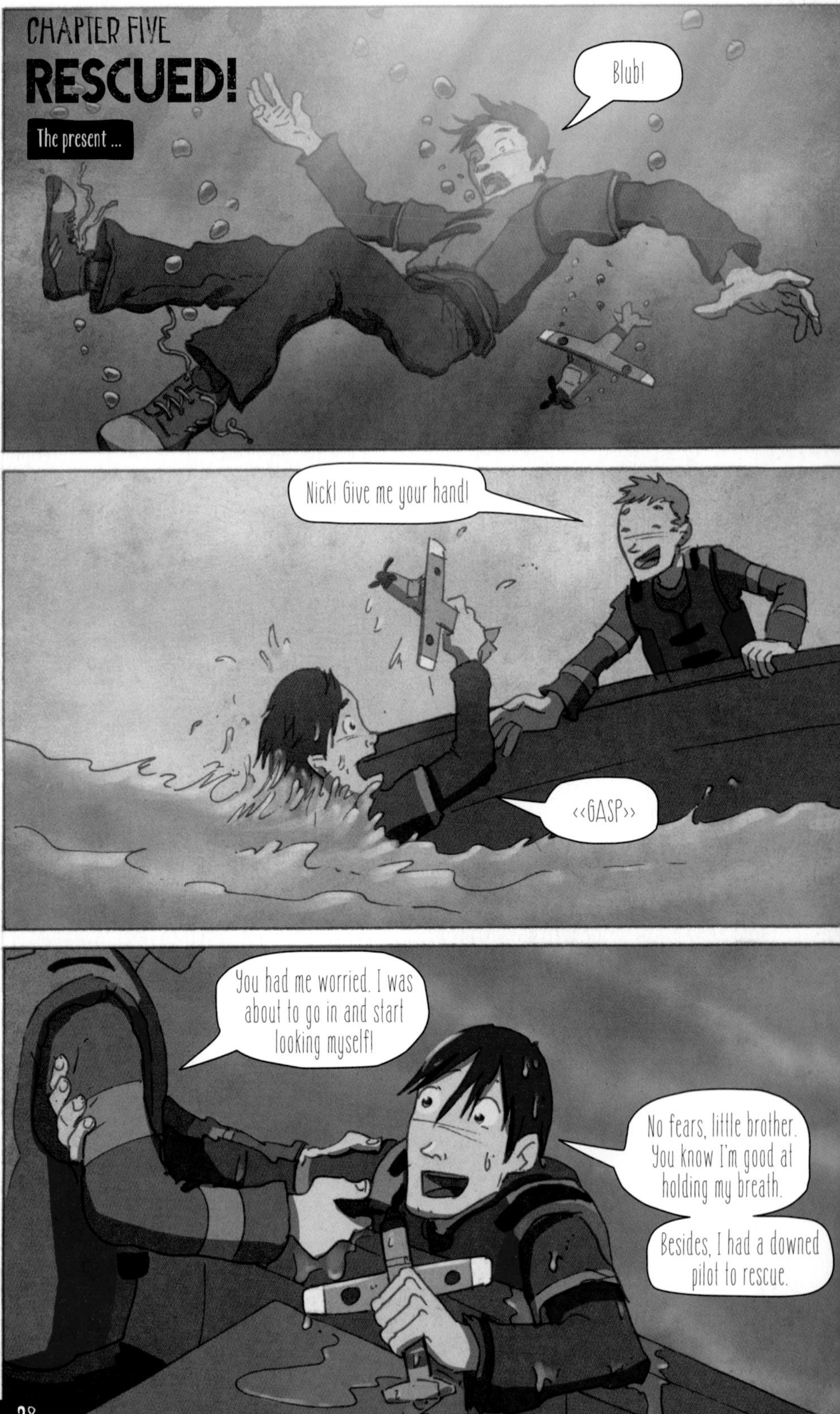
CHAPTER FIVE
RESCUED!
The present ...
Blub!
Nick! Give me your hand!
<<GASP>>
You had me worried. I was about to go in and start looking myself!
No fears, little brother. You know I'm good at holding my breath.
Besides, I had a downed pilot to rescue.

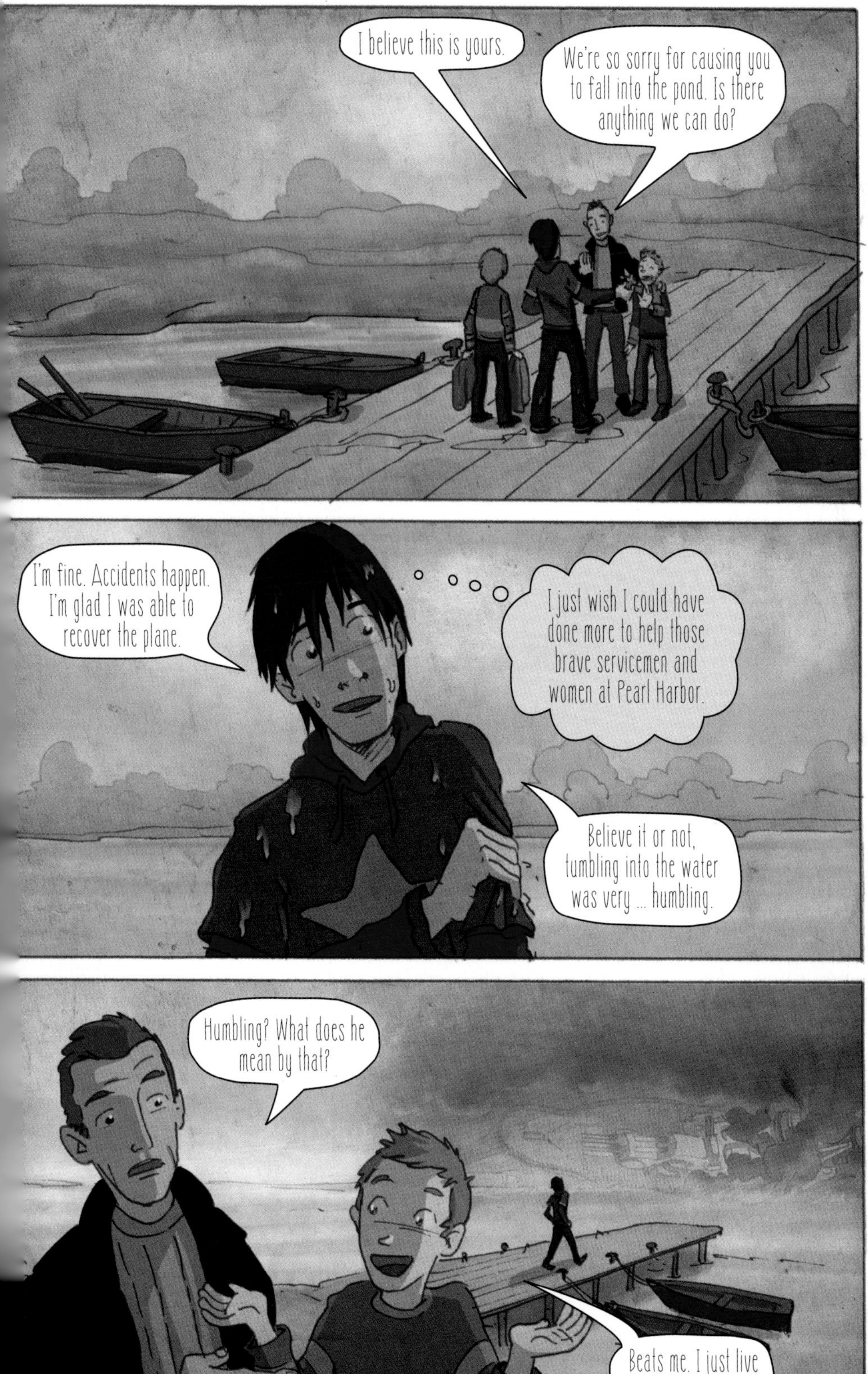
I believe this is yours.
We're so sorry for causing you to fall into the pond. Is there anything we can do?
I'm fine. Accidents happen. I'm glad I was able to recover the plane.
I just wish I could have done more to help those brave servicemen and women at Pearl Harbor.
Believe it or not, tumbling into the water was very ... humbling.
Humbling? What does he mean by that?
Beats me. I just live with the guy.

FLUX FILES

PLANNING THE ATTACK

The Japanese planned their attack on Pearl Harbor very well. Pilots spent days studying maps. War planners even created models of the harbor in large wading pools. The very day of the attack was even chosen on purpose. The Japanese thought the U.S. Navy would be less alert and unprepared to fight on a Sunday morning.

THE JAPANESE FLEET

The Japanese Navy's attack fleet consisted of six aircraft carriers, two battleships, three cruisers, eight destroyers, and several supply ships. They kept their fleet hidden out at sea. Then they launched the planes for the attack from this hidden location.

CASUALTIES

During the two-hour attack, a total of 2,335 U.S. service members died and 1,143 were wounded. Sixty-eight civilians perished, and 35 were wounded. The Japanese lost 65 men, with an additional soldier being captured.

MEATBALLS

The Japanese flew long-range Mitsubishi A6M Zero fighter planes during the attack. These planes had red circles painted on their sides. The circles represented the rising sun symbol from the Japanese flag. Americans often referred to these planes as "meatballs."

DECLARATION OF WAR

On December 8, one day after the attack, the United States declared war on Japan. U.S. President Franklin D. Roosevelt addressed the nation on the radio. He declared that December 7, 1941, would be "a date which will live in infamy."

REBUILDING AFTER THE ATTACK

During the weeks following the attack, the battleships *Pennsylvania, Maryland*, and *Tennessee* were put back into service. The *Nevada, California*, and *West Virginia* took years to repair, but they all eventually joined the active fleet. The *Oklahoma* and *Arizona* were damaged beyond recovery and did not return to service.

THE USS *ARIZONA* MEMORIAL

A memorial for the *Arizona* was built in 1962. It straddles the sunken hull of the battleship. More than 1 million visitors see the memorial each year.

GLOSSARY

AIRCRAFT CARRIER (AIR-kraft KAR-ee-ur)—a warship with a large flat deck where aircraft take off and land

BATTLESHIP (BAT-uhl-ship)—a warship outfitted with heavy armor and powerful guns

CAPSIZE (KAP-syz)—to tip over in the water

CIVILIAN (si-VIL-yuhn)—a person who is not in the military

DECLARATION (dek-luh-RAY-shuhn)—the act of announcing something, or the announcement made

FLEET (FLEET)—a group of warships under one command

HUMBLE (HUHM-buhl)—not boastful of one's own actions

INFAMY (IN-fuh-mee)—a lasting, widespread, and deep-rooted evil reputation brought about by something criminal, shocking, or brutal

ISOLATIONISM (eye-suh-LAY-shu-nism)—a policy of staying out of world affairs

MAGAZINE (MAG-uh-zeen)—a room aboard a ship where ammunition and explosives are stored

MEMORIAL (muh-MOR-ee-uhl)—something that is built or done to help people remember a person or event

MOBILIZE (MOH-buhl-ize)—to get troops and weapons ready for battle and put forces in place to do battle

MOOR (mor)—to secure by cables, ropes, or anchors

MULTIMEDIA (muhl-ti-MEE-dee-uh)—using or combining different kinds of communication technology, such as video, music, and printed text

SULFUR (SUHL-fur)—a yellow chemical element used in gunpowder, matches, and fertilizer

TORPEDO (tor-PEE-doh)—an underwater missile

READ MORE

ANTHONY, NATHAN, AND ROBERT GARDNER. *The Attack on Pearl Harbor in United States History.* In United States History. Berkeley Heights, N.J.: Enslow Publishers, Inc., 2014.

BENOIT, PETER. *The Attack on Pearl Harbor.* Cornerstones of Freedom. New York: Children's Press, 2013.

GARLAND, SHERRY. *Voices of Pearl Harbor.* Gretna, La.: Pelican Pub. Co., 2013.

KRIEG, KATHERINE. *The Attack on Pearl Harbor.* Perspectives Library. Ann Arbor, Mich.: Cherry Lake Publishing, 2013.

INTERNET SITES

FactHound offers a safe, fun way to find Internet sites related to this book. All sites on FactHound have been researched by our staff.

Here's all you do:

Visit *www.facthound.com*

Type in this code: 9781491402535

Super-cool stuff!

Check out projects, games and lots more at
www.capstonekids.com

INDEX

ABOUT THE AUTHOR

An award-winning newspaper reporter and columnist, Terry Collins now writes fiction, nonfiction, poetry, and graphic novels for readers of all ages. Some of his latest titles include biographies of Elvis Presley and Louis Armstrong, a historical fiction novel of Ancient China, and a graphic novel on the unsung heroes of World War II. A National Board Certified English instructor, he now teaches literature and creative writing in his hometown of Mount Airy, North Carolina. Despite a lack of shelf space for his ever-growing library, he will always believe a person can never have too many books.